MARIE LLOYD

&

MUSIC HALL

by Daniel Farson

Tom Stacey

ACKNOWLEDGEMENTS: The publisher would like to thank the author for his photographs and the ones lent to him by his many friends. They also acknowledge the photograph from Radio Times Hulton Picture Library, the *Observer*, Associated Newspapers and the Victoria and Albert Museum.

Published in 1972 by
Tom Stacey Ltd., 28-29 Maiden Lane,
London WC2E 7JP

ISBN 0 85468 082 9

Made and printed in Great Britain by
The Garden City Press Limited
Letchworth, Hertfordshire SG6 1JS

MARIE LLOYD and Music Hall

For *PETER BRADSHAW*

Contents

PART The Aftermath

List of Illustrations

PLATES

An early photograph of Marie Lloyd, wearing a floral hat and ringlets.
Marie in a grape-decorated hat holds two cherries in her mouth.
Marie poses with plumed headdress and parasol.

With Love to Ida Barr from Marie Lloyd

This portrait is inscribed to her friend Ida Barr.

'I followed on with my old cock linnet'—The stage props used when Marie sang 'My Old Man Said Follow the Van'.

Introduction

When I advertised for information about Marie Lloyd, as far back as 1964, I received an angry letter from Naomi Jacob.
She warned me that no one was 'allowed' to write about her friend except herself. It happened that she died soon afterwards,
but already I was determined to learn the truth about Marie Lloyd.

The truth, which has so many faces, is always hard to find; all the harder because Marie is so undocumented.
Macqueen Pope, her other biographer, largely repeated the well-intentioned inaccuracies of Naomi Jacob.

I believe that in trying to protect the woman they so admired, they did her a disservice. That in concealing the scandals and disasters of her life, they only diminished her.
It was Marie's courage in battling on that makes her remarkable.

When I first used the word 'scandal' in connexion with Marie Lloyd, Georgie Wood protested in *The Stage*: 'How dare' I say such a thing? But I was making no censure.
Undeniably she was scandalous in her time, but this was the fault of the time and not of Marie.

Naomi Jacob admitted that she 'purposely tried to avoid too much mention of those things which darkened the last years of her life.' She explained: 'to purposely omit these things is not of necessity to throw my picture of her out of drawing, to make it less true and less real'. I disagree; whitewash always obscures.

Marie never made excuses for herself – the Music Hall audiences never needed them.

Naomi Jacob prophesied: 'some day . . . a writer will set down for the generation of his or her time the true history of the Tragedy of Marie Lloyd.'

Much is revealed in that word 'Tragedy'.

Time has shown that it's not the tragedy, but the triumph of Marie Lloyd.

To understand Marie Lloyd, it's vital to
understand the background to Music Hall
and the years of conflict
out of which it was forged. It's important
to appreciate the craving for entertainment
that once existed in the East End of London –
both desperate and touching.

MARIE LLOYD.

WHIT MONDAY, 1893, DOUGLAS, ISLE OF MAN, FOR ONE MONTH. THEN STARRING PROVINCIAL TOUR UNTIL SEPT. 2

LONDON, SEPTEMBER 4.

EASTER, 1893, CANTERBURY, EMPIRE, TROCADERO, OXFORD.

CHRISTMAS 1892-93. THEATRE ROYAL, DRURY LANE.
PRINCIPAL GIRL, RED RIDING HOOD.
SOLE AGENT, THE OLD RELIABLE, GEO. WARE.

PART 1 The early days

1 The Pleasure Gardens

When Bethnal Green was green and the Isle of Dogs still marshland, the desire for entertainment was partly satisfied by the Pleasure Gardens. The splendid Vauxhall and Ranelagh, which charged an admission fee of a shilling and half-a-crown respectively, had their counterparts in the East End which were also elegant with trees, pagodas, fountains and statues, and ample space to wander in. Audiences may have been illiterate, but their capacity for enjoyment was staggering as they sat happily through hours of ballet, opera, and even Shakespeare performed in French.

A contemporary print of 'The Pleasure Grounds Eagle Tavern' looks surprisingly ornate; this is because a showman called Rouse had bought up the decorations of William IV's coronation in 1830. He also paid two aeronauts to ascend in a balloon from the Gardens and staged Devon and Cornish wrestling.

'The Eagle' had a colourful past and future. It started as a country pub called 'The Shepherd and Shepherdess' in the 1750s, and was replaced by 'The Eagle' in 1825 when the land was developed for the City Road. It figures in the song *Pop Goes the Weasel*: 'Up and down the City Road, in and out of The Eagle.'

In 1831, Rouse opened the 'Grecian Saloon' (also known as 'The Eagle' and 'The Old Greek') with an organ and automatic piano. Crowds flocked to stroll among the coloured lights and stare at the tight-rope walkers and other attractions, as many as six thousand people in one evening. When Victoria became Queen in 1837, Rouse built a covered walk around the Coronation Gardens, a new tavern, and a tent with a stage and still larger organ. Later he installed an orchestra and presented the East Enders with opera: *The Barber of Seville* and *Don Giovanni*. It was after this that it became known as 'The Royal Eagle Music Hall' and it seems to have suffered some decline. The land was sold to the Salvation Army when Marie was eleven, but with an irony the customers must have relished, General

Booth was not allowed to pull it down and had the frustration of seeing it continue with the evils of song and drink.

It was at 'The Eagle' that Marie studied her craft and made her first public appearance in 1885.

There were several such Gardens in the East End. In Hoxton, where Marie was born, The Rosemary Branch Gardens had a circus until the tent caught fire in 1852 killing seven horses and a troupe of performing dogs. But it must have continued in some form, for Marie was given a booking at 'The Rosemary Branch' on the same night as that first appearance at 'The Eagle'. There was also the 'Jews' Spring Garden in Stepney and the New Globe Pleasure Gardens in Mile End, which sported fireworks, concerts and more ascents by balloon. Sophie Von la Roche described the atmosphere of another Pleasure Garden at Sadler's Wells where people drank the water from the mineral springs: '. . . a playhouse dedicated to the small middle-class . . . lakes . . . numerous avenues with delightful tables and benches for visitors, under trees hung with tiny lamps. In the open temple, lassies, sailors and other young people were dancing.' The entertainment consisted of a comedy, a ballet, a rope-walker, mime, balancing tricks, a strong man and an operette. It lasted three hours. The audience refreshed themselves with wine, ham and pasties which they placed on the shelf that ran along the back of the seats in front of them.

The closest comparison I can conceive today is The Tivoli Gardens in Copenhagen. For years Joan Littlewood struggled to build her own Fun Palace somewhere in the East End but she has been defeated by local rules and regulations. Even if she had received planning permission, and raised the necessary millions, I wonder if the excellence of her ideas would have been appreciated.

As the population increased and space became more valuable, the Gardens declined. And just as the Pleasure Gardens fulfilled the promise of their name, so did the Penny Gaffs in the wretchedness of theirs.

2 The Penny Gaffs

The Gaffs were dense and dark. By poor people, for poor people, they were even closer to the origins of Music Hall. They flourished in the conditions of the East End and lasted until the 1880s, though a depressing 'penny pantomime' was seen in Whitechapel as late as 1904.

The Gaff was literally a theatre for a penny, held in a converted shop or stable. Garish pictures outside enticed the passers-by and the performance began when enough people had paid to go in, rather like the boxing-booths of a fairground. Reserved seats cost 2d. The show was a mixture of comedy, tragedy, farce, singing and dancing. It lasted for an hour and the Gaff closed at midnight after as many as six performances.

It was a rough and ready affair. The stage just a platform of boards and the orchestra a few German musicians perched on a table playing the fiddle, cornet, fife and flute. As many as 200 people sat on benches and when they were pleased they threw pennies on the stage to supplement the actor's nightly wage of 10d. Painted canvas served as the scenery and the act was lit by candles.

The majority of the audience was surprisingly young, from eight to twenty years old, and most of these were girls. Quick, as always, to suspect young people who were enjoying themselves, the establishment accused the Gaffs of being a training ground for thieves and pick-pockets. 'I have no doubt that a very large majority of those who afterwards find their way to the bar of the Old Bailey may trace their career in crime to their attendance at the Penny Theatre', wrote James Grant in 1830.

Though the comments of Blanchard Jerrold sound like the worst type of 'slumming', he explored most of London for his book with Gustave Doré, and knew the worst. He saw 'jollity' in the dens of Ratcliffe, but none here :

"The true Penny Gaff is the place where juvenile poverty meets juvenile crime. We elbowed our way into one that was the foulest, dingiest place of public entertainment I can conceive . . . The narrow passages were blocked by sharp-eyed young thieves, who could tell the policemen at a glance, through the thin disguise of private clothes . . .

' "This does more harm than anything I know of" said the sergeant, as he pointed to the pack of boys and girls who were laughing, talking, gesticulating, hanging over the boxes – and joining in the chorus of a song the trio were singing.

'An overwhelming cocked hat, a prodigious shirt collar, straps reaching half-way to the knees, grotesque imitations of that general enemy known to the Whitechapel loafer as a "swell", caricatures of the police, outrageous exaggerations of ladies' finery . . .

'The odour – the atmosphere – to begin with, is indescribable. The rows of brazen young faces are terrible to look upon. It is impossible to be angry with their sauciness, or to resent the leers and grimaces that are directed upon us as unwelcome intruders.

'Some have the aspect of wild cats. The lynx at bay,' concluded Jerrold with a dramatic flourish, 'has not a crueller glance than some I caught from almost baby faces.'

Even Henry Mayhew, in spite of his studies of the underworld, was shocked by the entertainment. This included a fourteen-year-old who danced with 'more energy than grace' and a comic in a battered hat who sang a song 'the whole point of which consisted in the mere utterance of some filthy word at the end of each stanza'. Mayhew admitted, 'nothing could have been more successful'. Another song called 'Pine-apple rock', with a rhyme that can be imagined, brought tears of 'enjoyment of the poison . . . it was absolutely awful to behold the relish with which the young ones jumped to the hideous meaning of the verses'.

There was even a 'drag' act – 'perfect in its wickedness'. Mayhew took it seriously : 'A ballet began between a man dressed as a woman, and a country clown. The most disgusting attitudes were struck, the most immoral acts represented, without one dissenting voice. If there had been any feat of agility, any grimacing, or in fact, anything with which the laughter of the uneducated classes is usually associated, the applause might have been accounted for; but here were two ruffians degrading themselves each time they stirred a limb, and forcing into the brains of the childish audience before them thoughts that must embitter a lifetime, and descend from father to child like some bodily infirmity.'

Like the later Music Hall, the Gaff was able to poke fun at the disasters of everyday life in the East End and so reduce them : 'The audience are delighted. Mr S reproaches Mrs S with the possession of a private gin bottle; Mrs S inveighs against the hideous turpitude of Mr S for pawning three pillow-cases to purchase beer. The audience are in ecstasies. A sturdy coal-heaver in the stalls slaps his thigh with delight. It is *so* real. Ugh! terribly real', wrote another squeamish observer, the journalist Augustus Sala.

Yet it sounds as if there was plenty of innocent enjoyment, and one visitor at least witnessed a moment of grace and gallantry. George Sims described how he paid 3d for a seat in a private box at 'The Garrick' in Leman Street, which was such a grand Gaff it was sometimes referred to later as a Music Hall.

'Two negroes, a sailor and a lady were the other occupants and they supped during the performance. Their supper, which consisted of trotters, was thrown up to them by a man in the pit who walked about and shouted his dainties. At the end of the play there was one trotter not eaten and this the sailor, carried away by his feelings, threw at the virtuous heroine as she spoke the tag. She picked it up, bowed her thanks to our box and carried it off with as much grace as a leading lady at the West End would have carried off a bouquet.'

Another time, an audience barracked a refined lady vocalist so cruelly, with catcalls and whistles, that someone shouted out – 'Give the poor old cow a chance, can't you !'

'Thank God' she called back gratefully, "at least there is *one* gentleman in the house.'

3 The Song and Supper Rooms

At the highest end of the social scale, far away from the Penny Gaff, were the 'Song and Supper Rooms' where the Chairman called on the customers to perform and encouraged the pace of the drinking. These offered excellent hot food and drink, as well as sophisticated entertainment which lasted into the early hours of the morning.

The most famous Supper Room was a mansion off Covent Garden which was sold by a Mr Joy to a Mr Evans, giving rise to the name 'Evans, late Joy's'. Evans set out to entertain the young gentlemen of the town in as lively a manner as possible. Dirty jokes and songs were encouraged, with elder sons hardly visible through the tobacco smoke as they banged their tumblers on the tables, demanding an extra chorus. Evans was succeeded by Paddy Green who made the place even more popular. It was visited by Edward VII when he was still Prince, who brought a party to hear Victor Liston sing a popular song of the moment ! *Shabby Genteel* :

> Too proud to beg, too honest to steal,
> I know what it means to be wanting a meal;
> My tatters and rags I try to conceal,
> I'm one of the shabby genteel.

Another favourite performer was Sam Cowell with his song *The Rat Catcher's Daughter* which he sang in the first Music Halls until he died from drink, particularly raw spirit consumed on a tour of America, in 1864 at the age of forty-five.

There was a curious fondness, among the 'highest in the land', for entertainment underground, as if they felt less guilty when they were beneath the surface of the earth. 'The Cave of Harmony' filled with a rush of MPs and Peers when Parliament finished for the night. Jerrold reported that 'members of both Houses, the pick of the Universities, and the bucks of the Row, were content to dwell in

• •

indecencies for ever. When there was a burst of unwonted enthusiasm, you might be certain that some genius of the place had soared to a happy combination of indecency with blasphemy.'

The most infamous Supper Room below ground was 'The Coal Hole' off the Strand, where curious mock Judge and Jury Trials were staged by Renton Nicholson, a self-styled Baron and wit. These investigated cases of seduction and breach of promise with men dressed up as women for the female witnesses. The result came close to an orgy. 'Everything was done that could be,' wrote a critic in 1858, 'to pander to the lowest propensities of depraved humanity.'

'The Lord Chief Baron Nicholson' moved on to 'The Cider Cellars' in Maiden Lane. By now, artists were interchanged as they were in Music Hall, and the most outstanding was W. G. Ross whose song about a chimney sweep on the eve of execution for murder caused such a sensation that crowds were turned away from the Cellars in the forties. Ross was billed as a 'character comedian' but this was high tragedy as remembered by Macqueen Pope's grand-father :

'He entered and did not start to sing right away. He was restless, his eyes darting about him but not seeing what they looked at. There was latent, controlled terror in every movement, realization of what every moment brought nearer. Instinctively, he took out his short clay pipe and lit it. Then his mood changed. A challenging bravado possessed him and gave him a rough, unnatural swagger. But not for long; realization came back, he fought it, and throwing himself in a chair he let his thoughts find utterance as he passed his life in review—'

> My name is Sam Hall, chimney sweep.
> My name it is Sam Hall.
> I robs both great and small,
> But they makes me pay for all,
> *Damn their eyes* !

The last line delivered with an unrepentant venom.

4 The Tavern and the Music Room

Between the Gaff and the Supper Room came the tavern for the vast majority. Most taverns of importance in both the West End and East End had a music licence.

It's easy to claim that the tavern was the parent of the hall and to name Charles Morton as the father. His 'Canterbury Arms at Lambeth is generally recognized as the first Music Hall, in 1849, though there are other contenders. But though Morton was the first impressario of Music Hall, he took advantage of a new law and exploited a situation that existed, he did not create it.

Another, more valid date for the birth of Music Hall was six years earlier, with the Theatres Act of 1843. This was the culmination of a hundred years of licensing madness.

Until then, theatres were not allowed to present plays (incredible though that sounds) except for 'Drury Lane' and 'Covent Garden' which enjoyed a Royal Charter. The 'minor' theatres of the East End, where they longed for straight drama, could only present plays in the guise of charity benefits or musicals. If they resorted to the subterfuge of a 'burletta' with songs and music, even their beloved Shakespeare could be staged. This had such ludicrous results as a performance of *Othello* with a musician playing a chord on the piano every five minutes, so softly it could hardly be heard. A Penny Gaff which dared to play *Othello* straight was raided by the police and the cast and the audience were taken to the police station and fined the next morning.

Consequently the law forced the 'minor' theatres into Variety. To make the whole thing still more absurd, the Royal theatres were so unsuccessful with straight drama that they plundered the East End theatres for the very acts they pretended to despise. Drury Lane featured performing lions and 'The Human Fly', a man who crawled all over the ceiling by means of suction.

Though they were denounced as a bad influence and a meeting

place for thieves and prostitutes, the East End theatres had no wish
to present obscenity – they were asking for the right to stage Shakespeare. All this dated from a Licensing Act as far back as 1737
which established the Lord Chamberlain as censor and decreed that
anyone who worked for gain in a place which didn't have a licence
from the King 'shall be deemed a rogue and vagabond'.

An actor called John Palmer fought the Act when he opened the
'Royalty Theatre' in Wellclose Square in 1787. The two Royal
theatres published an advertisement which stressed the penalties involved and scared off some of his actors, and the Society for the
Suppression of Vice protested against the 'revival of scenic
exhibitions' though the 'Royalty' was a graceful building holding
2,500 people and the play concerned was a 'benefit' of *As You Like
It*. Though the 'Royalty' was in one of the roughest parts of the East
End, the surrounding streets were choked with carriages by four
o'clock on the day of the opening. Palmer spoke to the audience
courageously : 'tumblers and dancing dogs might appear unmolested
before you, but other performers and myself standing forward to
exhibit a moral play is deemed a crime'. Sure enough, Palmer was
arrested under the Act, as a rogue, vagabond or sturdy beggar. He
met the magistrates in a public house and was so certain they were
going to send him to prison that he asked if he could fetch certain
documents. After a long wait, the magistrates discovered he had
locked them in. He was caught and released on bail, but the hostility
had become too much for him and he gave up the battle.

The unfortunate 'Royalty' reveals the extent of this hostility
against the theatre, which the halls inherited. The Church led the
attack and a middle-class God did his best to destroy the theatres by
fire. Over half the theatres of the East End were burnt until such
strict fire regulations were enforced that many of the smaller halls
couldn't afford the alterations and went out of business too. Around
200 Music Halls were closed after the 'Certificate of Suitability' Law
in 1878.

The 'Royalty' itself was burnt down in 1826. It was re-built as
'The Brunswick', but God made short work of that too. Its life must
be one of the briefest of any theatre in history.

The new 'Brunswick' had a splendid façade with walls 118 feet
high, but they were only two and a half bricks wide. Two days after
the opening, bits began to fall from the heavy iron roof until the
whole theatre buckled and collapsed killing fifteen people. The local

clergyman saw the disaster as an act of welcome retribution against the theatre in general, and 'The Royalty' in particular – that place where Palmer had dared to stage *As You Like It*.

Instead of a memorial, he gave a diatribe : 'Of late years the theatre that stood there was a most convenient focus of all the depravity of the most fearful neighbourhood in London.

'The effects of their guilt are too notorious and the enormity of their crimes was too vast not to make men tremble lest the wrath of God should visit the people in some general and awful manner.

'All this depravity was most fatally assisted by the late theatre. Indeed, it was a grand centre of abandoned publicans, Jews, crimps, brothel keepers, thieves and harlots with all the lowest and vilest who lived upon the plunder of sailors . . .

'The theatre necessarily and essentially draws round it all that is vile and guilty, as it is most convenient for all kinds of depravity – where the carcase is, there the eagles will be gathered together to feed on and destroy their prey.'

But in spite of the Church and the various busy-body committees dedicated to the suppression of vice, or what they called vice, the battle against the licensing laws was gradually gaining strength. Though Palmer had given up, others took his place.

Bulwar Lytton campaigned in Parliament and in 1832 supported one of the first resolutions to abolish the law. He attacked the monopoly 'which condemns the masterpieces of Shakespeare, whose very nature seems to scorn all petty bounds, fetters and limitations, to be performed at only two theatres, the only place, above all others, where they can least intelligently be heard'. He pointed out that the two proprietors didn't even make a profit, but enjoyed 'the monstrous satisfaction not only of degrading the drama but of ruining themselves'.

The East Enders also cared. When Sam Lane lost his licence at 'The Britannia' in Hoxton, for staging a straight production of *Black Eyed Susan*, he led a procession to Westminster with East Enders waving banners proclaiming ! 'Workers Want Theatres' and 'Freedom for the People's Amusement'. Today the East End theatres have closed through apathy and marches are made by dockers in protest against coloured immigrants.

The East End also used mockery. At the Christmas pantomime in 1831 at the Whitechapel 'Pavilion', a Major Monopoly attacked a Captain Minimus and suppressed him, but, as one critic reported :

'the monster enjoys but a short-lived triumph; he is in his turn attacked and destroyed to the great delight of the audience'.

Short-lived it most certainly was not, but in 1843 the Royal Monopoly was broken at last and under the new Act theatres were allowed to present plays.

One of the first was 'The Brit' at Hoxton, re-opened by Sam Lane who led the marchers. He told his audience: 'I am proud to have helped this success in obtaining freedom for the people's amusement. Never again will you be deprived of a free theatre. It has come to stay.' He kept to his word by staging the first British Shakespearian Festival with the special attraction of a different Hamlet every night.

5 The Tavern and the Hall

The licensing madness was over – but of course there were snags. Theatres had to be supervised by the Lord Chamberlain and were not allowed to serve food and drink. Taverns could serve food and drink but were no longer allowed to stage 'legitimate drama'. This was more drastic than it seems, for under the absurd restrictions many taverns had presented plays, like 'The King's Head' which gave scenes from *Othello* in 1839.

Now taverns had a choice. They could go 'legit' and become licensed theatres. Or they could stage the variety turns that the minor theatres were able to abandon. More and more taverns chose the latter and opened a music-room, concert-room, singing-room, or song-saloon in a hall beside the pub where they offered food, drink and song.

'Every publican', wrote Willson Disher, 'would now try to lay violent hands on the building next door, whether workshop or stable-yard, school or church. No opera house was too grand for the purpose and no shanty too mean.' So Music Hall was born.

Identities began to emerge. Some taverns chose to become theatres like 'The Effingham Saloon' which had been a favourite of sailors and prostitutes from the Ratcliffe Highway, offering rough entertainment at cheap prices. Now it became 'The Royal', offering 'opera bouffe' and a production of *Othello* with a different Moor for each act.

'The Brit', in Hoxton Street, whose licence had been refused, was so grand when it was rebuilt in 1858 that Charles Dickens exclaimed: 'I was in an immense theatre, capable of holding 5,000 people. What theatre? His Majesty's? Far better. Royal Italian Opera? Infinitely superior to the latter for hearing: infinitely superior to both for seeing in.'

Though 'The Brit' had chosen to become a theatre under the licence of the Lord Chamberlain, rather than a hall, Sam Lane's

widow kept up the music hall association with her Christmas pantomime and continued herself as the Principal Boy until the age of
seventy-six.

This pantomime became a favourite feature of London's Christmas; family audiences came down to the East End slums from all
over town and *King Klondyke* was seen by 260,000 people. Mrs
Lane invited Music Hall stars – Charles Coborn, Albert Chevalier,
and 'The Great Macdermott' who added a new word to the language
in 1877 with his rousing song 'We don't want to fight, but by Jingo
if we do'.

It was here, in 1888, when she was only eighteen, that Marie
Lloyd appeared as Princess Christina in *The Magic Dragon of the
Demon Dell*, a few yards from the street where she was born.

But most pubs seized the opportunity to present variety in a music
hall. 'By the beginning of the 1850s,' recorded A. E. Wilson, 'no public
house of pretension was complete without its song-saloon, licensed
for the purpose but forbidden to encroach upon theatrical preserves
by playing Shakespeare.'

'The Grapes' in Southwark Bridge Road, was the first tavern with
a singing-room (the Grand Harmonic Hall) to call itself a Music Hall
– 'The Surrey Music Hall'.

'The Mogul Saloon' in Drury Lane became the 'Middlesex Music
Hall' in 1851, though it was still referred to as 'The Old Mo'. 'The
Lord Nelson' in Whitechapel, 'The Lord Raglan' in Bloomsbury;
and 'The Green Gate Tavern' in the City Road, all became tavern
music halls in the 1850s. 'The Seven Tankards' and 'The Punch
Bowl' in Holborn, merged into 'Weston's Music Hall' in 1857. 'The
White Lion' in the Edgware Road was reconstructed as 'The Metro-
politan', and was one of the last to survive.

The transition was not peculiar to London. It happened all over
the country and is the justification for the claim that Music Hall
started in the pub.

6 Charles Morton – 'Father of the Halls'

Some northerners say that 'The Star Music Hall' in Bolton, originally a singing-room attached to the 'Millstones Inn', was the first true Music Hall. But it is Charles Morton who is generally recognized as The Father of the Halls, with the 'Canterbury Arms' at Lambeth.

Born in Hackney in 1819, Morton's first experience of the theatre came at 'The Pavilion' in Whitechapel where he sat among 'the sons and daughters of Israel and Jolly Jack Tars' according to his biographer Chance Newton. He graduated to the 'Garrick', the grand Gaff in Leman Street, and then 'The Cider Cellars', 'The Coal Hole', and especially 'Evans' Supper Room'.

At twenty-one he was married and the landlord of a Pimlico Pub where he started a free-and-easy for men only. Singers were locals or strollers who wandered from pub to pub and performed for a few shillings or their drinks. In December 1849 he took over the old 'Canterbury Arms' in Upper Marsh, Lambeth, transforming the pot house with mahogany tables and opened concerts for men on Mondays and Saturdays.

In 1852 he opened 'The Canterbury Hall', where a skittle alley had been, with a platform at the end as a stage. It held 700 people, opened every night, and allowed women though Morton sometimes discouraged them by pretending the house was full. Admission was gained by a 6d refreshment ticket, but part of this came back to the customer in drink. After three months the crowds proved so great that an extra 3d was charged at the door, and it is this entrance fee that supports the claim of the 'Canterbury' being the first real Music Hall.

Morton was a brilliant impressario, with a flair for publicity. He was ruthless in enticing artists away from the Supper Rooms where they received 30s a week, with the temptation of a salary of £30. His policy was: 'One quality only – the best.'

He brought E. W. Mackney, one of the first blacked-up Coons, from 'Evans' ' and billed him as 'The Great Mackney'.

'I wish you wouldn't do that,' Mackney protested, 'it makes me feel such a terrible sense of responsibility.'

'*You* be hanged,' said Morton. 'I pay you a salary, and all you are concerned with is doing your business to the best of your ability. It is *my* business to bill you in what I think is the best audience-attracting manner.'

Sam Collins was another regular until he opened his own Hall at Islington. But the most popular comic singer was Sam Cowell who turned up so late at 'Evans' ' one evening that Paddy Green sacked him on the spot : 'You've made him your God, gentlemen,' he told the audience, 'but he is not mine. He sings here no more.' Morton snapped him up.

But even Cowell took second place at the 'Canterbury' to the glee songs and madrigals sung by choristers to the accompaniment of a piano and vast harmonium. Morton catered to a refined audience of 'respectable mechanics and small tradesmen' with only a few 'fast clerks'.

The second 'Canterbury Hall' was opened in 1856 with a speed that would be unthinkable today. He started the expansion while the audiences were in, closed on a Saturday and re-opened with the splendid new building on Monday. Like so many of the Halls it was magnificent, astonishing. Curved staircases led elegantly to the balcony where customers looked down upon the stage and the rows of benches and tables with men wearing the inevitable top hats. There was an entrance hall with statues, an aquarium, and such a fine collection of pictures that it was known as 'The Royal Academy over the Water'. The entertainment rose to the occasion with selections of opera and the first English performance of Gounod's *Faust*, attracting music lovers from all over town.

Ironically, it was Morton's desire for culture, rather than variety, that caused him to fall foul of the Act of 1843, when he presented a Christmas 'Dramatic Sketch' in 1855. Now it was the turn of the theatres to prosecute, jealously guarding their hard-won rights. The Act was clear : 'A *performance* by any *two* men, singers or actors, constitutes a stage play, and can at once be put to a stop at a *music hall*'. As there were two speaking parts, Morton was fined £5 and the performance stopped. The author then produced another version in which he played all the parts himself, and this time the law was powerless.

The next trouble occurred when Morton staged a condensed version of *The Tempest*—for the appetite for Shakespeare was insatiable. Not only did his leading actor break a blood vessel and die, but rival theatrical managers brought proceedings against him. 'I am sorry indeed, to have to fine you for the production of such a splendid novel and pleasant entertainment,' said the magistrate, 'but the law is very strong on this point; and enacts that you shall not perform a stage play, or any part of it, in an unlicensed place.''

Morton was fined £5 again, but gained from the publicity of a full report in *The Times*. This prompted him to ask *The Times* to accept an advertisement, the first from a Music Hall.

Litigation under the Act of 1843, between theatres and halls, continued into this century. In February 1861, a converted saloon in Piccadilly was opened as 'The London Pavilion', and Morton invaded the West End a month later with 'The Oxford' on the site of the 'Boar and Castle Inn' at the corner of Oxford Street and Tottenham Court Road (later but no longer a Lyons Corner house). This cost £35,000 – 'Not only the place for music and amusement; but a place to lunch, dine, and sup at till one o'clock in the morning.' At the 'Canterbury', you could have a dozen oysters – or a chop and baked potato – for a shilling.

Morton's luck changed. The 'Oxford' burnt down in 1868 and though it was rebuilt he had nothing more to do with it. When he took over a theatre in Islington, rival theatrical managers started proceedings when he ran Music Hall. Instead of fighting them, he joined them, and re-opened 'The Philharmonic Music Hall' as a legitimate theatre where he staged an 'opera bouffe', *La Fille de Madame Angot* with great success. But when he took it to America in 1874, he lost £8,000.

Managing 'The Alhambra', Leicester Square (now the Odeon Cinema), for eleven years, Morton presented the top stars including Marie Lloyd. He moved to the 'Tivoli' in the Strand and then to 'The Palace' where he showed the latest Boer War films on a biograph. He presented Marie on Boxing Day 1897.

By the time he was eighty, he was venerated as the founder of Music Hall. A tribute from Clement Scott shows how extravagantly he was honoured :

What has he done for us, Grand Old Man!
In his record of Eighty Years?
He has fought for Liberty! Planted Truth!
With trouble, maybe with tears!

The tribute goes on to refer to the drinking dens of seventy years
ago:

The jokes they made and the songs they sang
Were sorrow to Englishmen
But he dreamed of the madrigal, Grand Old Man,
And the English catch and glee,
And murmured 'Pleasure it should be pure, and Art it must
    be free.'
So he opened a sing-song bright and gay,
Vice took to its heels and ran!
Said the women 'Oh Governor! Let us in!'
'You shall come' said the Grand Old Man.

The next verse refers to his scuffles with the Act of 1843 –

'So they dug old Acts of Parliament up, and tinkled the
    legal bell'

But all ended happily :

Then they left the Grand Old Man alone,
Safe planted, firm on feet.
And now if they pine for nastiness,
They must go down another street.
They have swept it out of the Music Halls;
And Variety lifts her head.
With the aid and fame of a Liberal Man,
Now the Dog in the Manger's dead!

A truly awful verse, revealing the first warnings of the respectability
to overcome Music Hall. It's odd that such an abstemious man
should have been involved with Music Hall in the first place 'in his
youth he never applied hot and rebellious liquors to his blood' wrote
Chance Newton. Morton died six years later, but his place was taken

by a still more dedicated champion of gentility – Oswald Stoll. Alarmingly, he was a teetotaller too, and became an adversary of Marie Lloyd in his urge to make Music Hall respectable.

By the time Marie was born, Music Hall was established and flourishing. There were more than 300 halls throughout the country. The entertainment seems so innocent today, but then it was condemned by the staid middle-class as the sinful successor to the Penny Gaff and Cider Cellar. Marie found that she had to pay for the scandalous reputation of Music Hall itself. To many people, she *was* Music Hall.

7 The East End and the Cockney

Both Marie and the Music Hall grew up in conditions peculiar to their time.

Writers referred to 'the people of the abyss', 'the destitute' and 'submerged' – solemn but true. Overcrowding was so bad that ten to fifteen thousand men, women and children roamed the streets at night and slept out. Others shared a 4d bed, sleeping in shifts. Houses containing twenty-four people were built on dustheaps and the smell from the refuse below combined with the stink from the gutters to poison an air already stale from over-use.

Work houses cared for 128,000 people. There were a hundred hospitals, a hundred refuges, fifty orphan asylums, eighteen penitentiaries for fallen women, forty homes for poor sailors ... twelve for poor Jews. The conditions inside can be imagined.

Prostitution was inevitable. Three thousand brothels were listed officially and there were at least 80,000 prostitutes or 'lost women' in London altogether.

Curiously, there was little discretion or concealment. They crowded the heart of the capital as soon as darkness fell and flocked to the Music Halls in search of trade.

The Haymarket, so dull today, was full of people then : 'Men and women jostling each other, many of both sexes being intoxicated ... beggars solicit us at every crossing ... the cafés are overflowing with Gauls from across the channel ... a stranger cannot help being astonished at the vast, almost incalculable number of unfortunate women who haunt the London streets in this quarter as the hour of midnight approaches.' This was the startled impression of a genteel American writer, Daniel Kirwan, published the year that Marie was born. London was swollen with people.

At the beginning of the century the population was 865,000; by 1851 it was nearly 1,400,000; then the city burst and by 1888 it was

MARIE LLOYD THE EARLY DAYS

and Music Hall

over four million. That was the year of Jack the Ripper and the East End was his easy pitch, where the cry of murder was so common it was barely noticed.

If the West End was continental, the East End, where Marie was born, was a maelstrom of the world. Chinese were tunnelling their warrens in Limehouse; Lascars walked up West India Dock Road with brown paper parcels; there were Swedes in Spitalfields; and Russians and Polish Jews settled in so many thousands around Whitechapel that in some streets it was a surprise to hear English spoken. Astonishingly the immigrants were easily absorbed. Unlike America, there was little problem of a criminal second generation. They endured their poverty with patience, humour and hard work. They became proudly British yet clung to their own traditions which can still be found in Whitechapel and Commercial Road with Jewish shops and Kosher restaurants; Sunday markets, like Petticoat Lane for clothes and Hessel Street for food; a Yiddish Theatre with plays in Hebrew; and an off-licence called 'The House of Frumkin' where they used to offer a glass of cherry brandy and a slice of cake as you made your order.

Today we are hardly aware that London has a port. Then it was one of the most dissolute ports in the world, stretching for miles with fingers of docks reaching into the ship-littered Thames. Sailors of every nationality poured ashore, prosperous after their time at sea, eager for drink, sex and fun – and were quickly robbed.

In the days of Marie's childhood, the waterfront was seething with a tangle of taverns, dens and kitchens. Gustave Doré has engraved a night scene which conveys the atmosphere of hidden violence, of people fighting outside a lighted doorway, a figure slumped on the ground, another slouching away watched by two small girls, a solitary dog, a man asleep or drunk on a barrow, a forest of masts in the background, the whole scene illuminated by a full moon. Describing this as: 'the pitched battle we witnessed outside a public-house at Dockhead one threatening night', his collaborator Blanchard Jerrold warns of the strong dislike in Ratcliffe to people who came from the West End of London because their wealth 'would be regarded as aggressive and impertinent in these regions upon which the mark of poverty is set in lively colours'.

Jerrold appreciated the rollicking nature of the poverty: 'Jack gives a constant jollity to the scene – and is the occasion of the interminable roistering apparent in lines of low public houses thronged with ragged, loud-voiced men and women.'

But most observers were shocked. Closely guarded by a policeman, the American Daniel Kirwan also came to Ratcliffe, supposedly named from the red cliffs that once lined the shore. He saw no jollity. He described 'The White Swan', known locally as 'Paddy's Goose', as 'perhaps the most frightful hell-hole in London. The very sublimity of vice and degradation is here attained, and the noisy scraping of wheezy fiddles, and the brawls of intoxicated sailors are the only sounds heard within its walls. It is an ordinary dance house, with a bar and glasses, and a dirty floor on which scores of women of all countries and shades of colour can be found dancing with Danes, Americans, Swedes, Spaniards, Russians, Negroes, Chinese, Malays, Italians and Portuguese in one wild hell-medley of abomination.'

Ratcliffe Highway was probably the roughest street in London. This reputation was inherited by Cable Street, the parallel road above. Today Cable Street has been 'cleaned up' and the Highway is wide and empty.

The influence of the river permeated the Halls and Theatres. Because of the sailors, 'nautical drama' was a popular feature especially at 'The Pavilion', Whitechapel which was advertised as 'The Great Nautical Theatre of the Metropolis'. Jews and sailors relished such productions as 'The Sailor's Home' with 'Naval engagements and picturesque tableaux'. *The Referee* described an audience in 1883 : 'It is perhaps the most cosmopolitan pit in the metropolis. Here may be seen the bluff British tar; the swarthy foreign sailor fully arrayed in a picturesque sash, a red mop-cap and a pair of ear-rings; the Semitic swell in glossy broadcloth and the rorty coster, a perfect blaze of pearly buttons . . .'

Another East End theatre destroyed by fire in 1866 was 'The Standard', Shoreditch which rose again as 'the largest and most magnificent Theatre in the world' where nearly every actor, including Irving, appeared. Ballet amazed with 150 fairies floating in the air, and spectacle astonished with a real horse-race that galloped in from one side and out the other into Holywell Lane while a police-man stopped the traffic. 'Nautical dramas' included the sinking of the Princess Alice in the Thames, with dead bodies laid out on the stage. This was a real accident which the East Enders remembered with emotion. Small boys re-created the waves by stirring about under a painted canvas.

MARIE LLOYD
and Music Hall

Though it was illegal, men still searched the two thousand miles of sewers for old iron, metal or money, risking the nauseous gasses and the swarms of rats, some as big as kittens. Mudlarks combed the river at low tide and a few plundered the water itself for dead bodies, the reward that went with them, and rings on their fingers.

With true Victorian paradox, the riches of the East flowed through all this poverty down the West India and East India Dock Roads. Joseph Conrad in *Chance*, described the corner where the roads met, with vans 'swaying like mountains' and 'the inhabitants of that end of the town where life goes on unadorned by grace or splendour; they passed us in their shabby garments, with sallow faces, haggard, anxious or weary, or simply without expression, in an unsmiling sombre stream not made up of lives but of mere unconsidered existencies whose joys, struggles, thoughts, sorrows and their very hopes were miserable, glamourless, and of no account in the world.'

Conrad failed to see that there *had* to be glamour in such surroundings. The cockney found it in Music Hall, which offered him magic, drink, women, and escape.

The cockney was an extraordinary character – then. He was strong enough to be gentle. He could afford to indulge in an unashamed sentimentality. As well as the law of the jungle there was a sort of chivalry, a gallantry and the saving grace of laughter.

This spirit existed also in the North and there were halls throughout the country for people who were equally poor. But the East End had a special affinity with Music Hall because of this defiance of life that the halls shared, and portrayed.

Hoxton, where Marie was born, was listed officially as 'Hoxton New Town', but it was rich and rough in such entertainment. The 'Brit' hovered between variety and drama, and there was Macdonald's on the other side of the street which opened as the 'Hoxton Music Hall' in 1863. It ended up as a mission hall and still exists today, used for the occasional Music Hall show.

Another hall opened in Pitfield Street three years before Marie was born, holding a thousand people. 'The Virgo' acquired a reputation that belied its name. A. E. Wilson mentions it in his book on East End Entertainment: 'Its patrons were of the roughest kind and the hall was popularly known by a term which is too offensive to sully these

Evans Music Hall: The late-night song and supper room in Covent Garden. Engraving from 'London at Play'.

'Up and Down the City Road, In and Out the Eagle.' Marie made
her first professional appearance here in 1885 under the name of
Bella Delmere.

The Falling of the New Brunswick Theatre.

fair pages. 'The . . .'s opera' is as near as I can represent it, the blank being occupied by a word of similar meaning to that which Johnson in his dictionary defined as a "term of endearment among sailors." '

The word is plainly 'sod'. The phrase 'Sod's Opera' is still used by sailors today to describe a bawdy, drunken sing-song, and probably that is all that happened in Pitfield Street.

This part of London was Marie's birthplace. In one way, the slums of Hoxton were a devastating background for a child, but it was far richer in human experience than the dull, tall towers that dwarf the East End today.

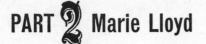

8 Matilda Wood

Marie Lloyd was born on 12 February 1870 as – Matilda Alice Victoria Wood. It was the same year that Charles Dickens died. At first it's hard to understand why she meant and still means so much.

She won few honours in her lifetime, no badges of officialdom like the knighthoods for Robey and Lauder, the Legion of Honour for Little Tich, or the CBE for Gracie Fields. Nor did she achieve any of the respectability of her rival Vesta Tilley who married an impressario and ended up as Lady de Frece. Marie's third husband was a troublesome jockey who was half her age and knocked her about.

Tilley retired in triumph in 1920 at 'The Coliseum' where she was presented with the signatures of two million admirers and so many flowers that it took several vans to carry them home. Marie could not afford a farewell appearance and was considered too great a risk for 'The Coliseum'.

Edward VII admired her, but her reputation became so scandalous that she was barred from the first Royal Command Performance, held especially for Music Hall in 1912.

She was arrested in New York with the young jockey, and interned on Ellis Island as an 'undesirable'.

Lovely as a child, she aged rapidly and sadly.

Her hair was poor, her teeth protruded.

She was hot-tempered, impulsive, extravagant in everything she did – and she drank. Yet Marie Lloyd was the most radiant star of Music Hall. And she was something more – a spirit of rebellion when this was unfashionable – and took courage. She defied the Establishment and 'they' tried to destroy her.

But Music Hall was a people's entertainment, by them and for them. The performer more important than the performance. Marie sang of things they knew about, like booze and bailiffs, and let them laugh. All her life she had a rare sympathy with the audience – all the honour, all the love she needed came from them.

Legend has it that she was born prophetically in Peerless Street. But legend as far as Marie is concerned, has always been inaccurate. The real address was far more down to earth, and appropriate — 36 Plumber Street. Matilda was the name of her mother (who also called herself Maud) and signed the birth certificate with her 'mark'. Marie was the first of nine children, and took full advantage of her seniority. 'Even as a child', said her sister Anne, 'she was always the leader of everything, not only that went on in our house but with all the kids that lived in the street.' She told me how Marie scrubbed the babies in their tin bath with such force that her mother had to object. Also, of the old German woman who lived next door. Always mischievous, Marie was exploring the roofs of the houses and found herself peering through a skylight into Mrs Schultz's kitchen. The German woman was frying sausages with a long, pronged fork when she happened to look up, saw Marie, screamed and upset the fat which caught fire on the stove. Seeing the flames and the fork, as if she was looking down into hell, Marie also started to scream and lost her footing. She fell through the skylight in a shower of glass on top of the German woman and ran out of the house still screaming.

Financially they were poor, but a happy and united family. This was due to Mrs Wood, ample, humorous, shrewd – a typical cockney. She provided the incentive, urging the children on. She was clever at dress-making and house-proud. Marie inherited this passion for cleanliness until it was almost an obsession. The more disorderly her life became, the more the house had to be spotless. Her maids were given strict orders to see that the rooms were free of dust – 'cleanliness was a God to Marie' recalled her sister Anne. 'Everything was always shining. "Look after the corners" she'd say, "and the middle will look after itself." '

John Wood, the father, was popular but unambitious. He made artificial flowers for an Italian who exploited him shamelessly and though he invented a rose with a smell, he was only paid thirty shillings a week.

The Wood children made their own amusement, and were organized by Marie. Births and weddings were commonplace, unless Royal, but death was an occasion. Marie and sister Alice would take a penny-halfpenny bus ride to the end of the line where there was a

MARIE LLOYD

and Music Hall

cemetery and gape at the pomp and pageantry so absent in Plumber Street. On a good day, they saw as many as eight funerals.

She drilled her sisters into forming a Minstrel troupe, all the rage then, and while her brother sold programmes, the Fairy Bell minstrels toured the local missions with a sketch on the evils of drink. Alice was the long-suffering wife and Marie played the husband who had sworn 'to eat his hat' if he ever drank again. Crying out – 'Ten o'clock and he is not yet home. He will be drunk!', Alice cooked an old straw hat and served it to Marie when she staggered in, wearing her father's coat, demanding supper. Choking on the bits of straw, Marie then sang her first song: 'Throw down the bottle and never drink again.' Sadly unprophetic.

Marie's first taste for Music Hall came through her father's part-time job as a waiter at the 'Royal Eagle Tavern'. He was popular and known as 'Brush' Wood because he carried a small brush and dusted himself down after serving.

Several times he brought his daughter to watch the entertainment. She described her impressions later: 'Every time I saw the performers dance I thought I could do better, and as for their singing it struck me, as it does for all youthful aspirants for stage honours, that my voice was superior to theirs. And in order to prove the possession of that superiority, as I could not get an audience that would pay to see me dance and hear me sing, I would get all my young sisters, even the last baby sister, to go into the coal cellar or up to the back attic, and have them witness my grand and expert gyrations, and listen to my beautiful voice. It must have been beautiful, for every time I sang they would all try to join in with a very primitive and somewhat nasty chorus in which their yells would denote that they also possessed voices, probably not so sweet and beautiful as mine, but voices and lungs just the same. Even our blessed kid of six months old would join in and howl with delight, at least I always imagined it was with delight till my mother would come down to the cellar and sternly ask me 'What are you doing with the poor baby?''

If Marie was ten, the audience would have consisted of: Johnny (9) Alice (7), Grace (5), Daisy (3) and the baby Anne (6 months). The children had an instinctive flair for entertainment: Alice and Grace formed The Lloyd Sisters in 1888; Rosie Lloyd formed the Lloyd Family with Marie Lloyd junior; and Daisy Wood had a long successful career in the Halls as well. As children they made a perfect supporting cast for Marie.

Her mother tried to check Marie's wild spirits by getting her a job. The first, making boots for babies, lasted a week. At the next job the other girls dared her to dance on the table while the forewoman was out of the room. There was a lively clash when she returned unexpectedly.

'Is this what happens when you're left alone for a moment?' she asked.

'I couldn't very well do it while you were in the room, could I?' said Marie, to which there was no answer but the sack. She broke the news when she returned home that night, with the comforting announcement that she wanted to go on the stage. 'At first my parents raised an objection, but when they saw that they couldn't kick their objections as high as I could kick my legs, they very sensibly came to the conclusion to let things take their course and said to me ! "Bless you my child, do what you like." '

Calmly, her mother offered to help her with her costume. She understood Marie's ambition. Years later, referring to her own daughter, Marie said, 'I s'pose it's in the blood. If my mother had gone on the stage she'd have shown them something. But she didn't, you see. She contented herself with bringing us up and bringing us out. She's always suggesting and criticizing, is Ma.'

Her father arranged for her first appearance at 'The Grecian' (or 'Old Greek', attached to 'The Eagle') in a week which included Jenny Hill 'The Vital Spark' and Herbert Campbell, two of the leading artists of the day.

On Saturday night, 9 May 1885, at the age of fifteen, she was added as an extra turn under the name of 'Bella Delmere'. There are various spellings for this – Bella Delmare – Naomi Jacob; Belle Delamere – Macqueen Pope in *The Melodies Linger On*; Bella Delmore – Macqueen Pope in *Queen of the Music Halls*; Bella Delmere – Willson Disher and Colin Macinnes; I choose the last because Disher is the most accurate authority.

She rose to the robust atmosphere of Saturday night and gloried in it, at a salary of half-a-crown. 'I was in luck too. For a gentleman in front promptly engaged me to appear that same evening at the 'Rosemary Branch' in the New North Road. So with another half-crown in view I packed up my little bundle of stage clothes, slung it across my back, like Dick Whittington in search of a bloody fortune ! You see, I had no nerves in those days.'

Raw, naïve, pinching other artists' songs without permission, her appeal was immediate. She took to Music Hall as if she was born to it. Within a few weeks she was spotted by an agent who urged her to change her name from the la-di-dah Delmere to something more simple. There are various versions of this story : of the agent looking out of his window and noticing a placard advertising Lloyd's Weekly; of Marie seeing a poster in the street of 'The Family Oracle', a kindly old man raising a hand to stress some point while he clasped a copy of Lloyd's in the other. 'Marie' was chosen as posh and slightly French. In fact, few names could have been simpler than her own – Matilda Wood – but from now on it was Marie Lloyd and she appeared under that name on 22 June. Most of the sisters adopted it too.

Marie dated the start of her career from her appearance at 'The Falstaff Music Hall' in Old Street, where she was spotted by a manager called George Belmont, it all happened so quickly. On 17 August she was fourth on the bill at 'The Star Palace of Varieties', a popular hall at Bermondsey, after the comic Tom Leamore. I have seen her wage-packet for the week : fifteen shillings. She 'borrowed' a song from Nelly Power – *The Boy in the Gallery* – and made it into a favourite of her own. Unlike most Music Hall songs, it's a simple, beautiful ballad with a wistful charm that still captivates today.

> The boy I love is up in the gallery,
> The boy I love is looking now at me,
> There he is – can't you see
> Waving his handkerchief
> As merry as a robin
> That sings on the tree.

Nelly Power died two years later at the age of thirty-two, and was so poor that the undertaker sued her agent George Ware for £8.19.6 for the funeral expenses. Later Ware acted as agent for Marie.

At the beginning of 1886, Marie went to Ireland at £10 a week. In September she appeared regularly at the 'Sebright Music Hall' in a very mixed bill which included : 'Sergeant Simms Zouave Troupe; the King of Egypt; a one-legged champion; Marie Lloyd and others.' There was a note that no artist was allowed to appear without producing proper 'assignments for songs' beforehand, but by now Marie was more scrupulous in buying her songs. These included : *Harry's a Soldier; She has a sailor for a lover; And the leaves began to fall; Sure to Fetch Them;* and *Oh Jeremiah, don't you go to sea* a popular number written by an old man who was blind and dictated his songs to his daughter. Two special favourites were *Whacky-Whack* and *When you Wink the Other Eye* – the start of Marie's famous wink to the audience.

On 23 October she received one of her first reviews. *The Era* reviewed a bill at 'The Paragon', where Marie appeared with Little Tich, and described her as 'Miss Marie Lloyd, a pretty little soubrette who dances with great dash and energy'.

By the end of 1886 she played several Halls a night, travelling between them by horse and brougham. Now she was earning a hundred pounds a week. In just over a year the barefoot girl from Hoxton had become a public idol and a rich woman, at the age of sixteen. The transition was shattering and she never recovered. It may explain her generosity, which became wild and compulsive as if she felt a secret guilt over her sudden success.

9 Percy Courtenay – the First Mr Lloyd

Marie married her first husband, Percy Courtenay, the following year (not 'Courtney' as usually stated). They had been introduced by a mutual friend who was sweet on Marie himself and recorded his mistake by writing a rueful ballad 'Never introduce your donah to a Pal.'

Never thinking twice about anything, she accepted Courtenay's proposal impulsively. She looked up to him as an experienced man of the world – he was a ripe twenty-five year old but she discovered all too soon that he was a gentleman of leisure for the simple reason that he didn't work. Describing himself on official documents as a General Dealer or Commission Agent, he was really a race-course tout. When his luck was in, he was extravagant and this must have impressed Marie at first.

They married on 12 November 1887 at the St John the Baptist Church in Hoxton. Courtenay's father was described as Captain Edward Courtenay and John Wood still called himself an artificial florist while Mrs Wood signed with her 'mark'. Marie gave her age as eighteen, instead of seventeen, and left a blank under the heading of 'Profession', presumably for the sake of respectability. The couple moved into a grand house in Lewisham, with four maids in uniform and a large St Bernard called Bob – another staggering change in Marie's early life.

Courtenay is only remembered as a shadowy figure. It seemed unlikely, more than eighty years later, that I should find anyone who knew him. Surprisingly, such a person existed in Brinsworth House at Twickenham, a home for retired Music Hall artists. My spirits sank as I was led to a clean room where a few old people sat in armchairs or shuffled across the polished floor, but they rose when I met Flo Hastings, the person I came to see. She was a teenage girl friend of Marie when both were enjoying the first excitement of success; now she was ninety-seven, and since then has celebrated her 100th birthday. She seized one of the old song-sheets I'd brought for her and peered at her picture on the cover 'Oh look! How pretty I was before the moths got at me. Did you know, years ago I had all London at my feet? I bought five stage dresses off Marie, beautiful they were! Twenty-five shillings for the lot. Her mother was *so* annoyed, she slapped Marie's face.' Flo Hastings chuckled, 'Her mother was a very plain woman.'

I asked about Courtenay and for a terrible moment I thought her memory had failed her and she was confusing him with Marie's third husband, Bernard Dillon, the jockey. In fact her memory was exceptional; it was simply that the first and third husbands came full circle — the similarity of the two men was astonishing.

'Courtenay? Oh yes, I remember him' she said with disgust. 'Handsome? No, but smartly dressed. He was slim, not a big man. He was a racing man you know, used to hang around the race course — a punter.

'I used to sleep with Marie when he was away in the West End with his racing friends. He was always out with other women. He'd ask her for fifty pounds and swear he'd make it up tomorrow, but she'd never see it again. She hated him.' The memories rushed back. 'Oh he was a dirty old thing. One night at the 'Standard' (later the 'Victoria Palace') he came up to me and used filthy language just as I was going on. I flung a drink in his face and the barman nearly killed him — the dirty thing.'

'Why was Marie attracted to him?'

'God knows.' For a few seconds Flo Hastings was silent. 'She was a silly woman really, always after the men. But then she was thrown into all this and muddled up. Fellows coming after her all the time.' Her tone softened. 'Oh she was lovely! She told me "Look Flo, if you need any money send for me, nobody else." We'd go out at night, just the two of us and be so happy.' She sighed. 'She was a pal. The sweetest woman in the world.'

Another girl was even closer to Marie — Bella Orchard who became Bella Burge, and appeared on stage as Bella Lloyd. Always stage-struck, though never a star, she had a tiny part as a fairy queen in the Christmas pantomime at 'The Pavilion', Whitechapel in 1889. Alice and Grace, as the Sisters Lloyd were on the same bill and invited Bella home for tea. Home was Marie's house at Lewisham, already a communal meeting-place for the entire Wood family. Marie's inability to live with one person only, her need for a constant crowd of hangers-on must have infuriated Courtenay. Her

famous Sunday parties were 'open house' for the Music Hall profession, apart from such real friends as Gus Elan, Dan Leno, and
Eugene Stratton. Courtenay poured their drinks in it all, but sadly
out of it.

Marie and Bella took to each other immediately. The next day
Marie saw Bella's mother, who had remarried, and unofficially
'adopted' her as companion and dresser. Bella moved in and
Courtenay had the additional irritation of a spy under his own roof.
Marie was nineteen and Bella thirteen. It was a strange arrangement.

Flo Hastings told me how she used to sleep in the house and
Leslie Bell, in *Bella of Blackfriars*, describes how Bella would 'wake
up and find that she was sharing her bed with one or two other young
women. Marie would never send a friend away while there was room
to be found in the house, but she seldom woke Bella while making her
theatrical companions at home for the night, simply rolling her
gently to one side of the bed. Occasionally, Bella would be only
drowsy when Marie returned and would open her eyes to see a pair of
bright blue ones twinkling down into her own and hear Marie's voice
softly say : "Shove over love, you've got company." '

In whose bed was Courtenay? Yet a baby daughter was born and
named after Marie, poor Marie Junior whose only success in life
came from impersonations of her famous mother, with whom she
had so little in common. Even when she was five, a journalist describing a visit to Marie's home wrote 'The most interesting feature of
the impromptu drawing-room entertainment was furnished, however, not by Miss Lloyd but by her tiny girl who, with a curious
fidelity, reproduces every word and every gesture of mama.'

Even the birth of a daughter made little difference to the marriage.
Courtenay had a habit of returning from the races to the bar of one of
the Halls where Marie was appearing. Celebrating his wins, or, more
often, drowning his losses, he caused such a disturbance that Bella
often had to call for the police. By 1893, Marie and Courtenay were
living apart; this was legalized by a deed executed on 23 January
1894. Characteristically, it was Marie who moved out of their house.

In May of that year, around nine o'clock on the evening of the
10th, Marie left the stage door of 'The Empire' in Leicester Square
and Courtenay rushed at her with a stick, shouting dramatically –
'You are not going into that brougham tonight. I will gouge your
eyes out and ruin you.' While Bella tried to stop him, Marie ran back
into the safety of the theatre and the door-keeper blocked his way.

But after ten minutes, even more afraid of arriving late at the next Music Hall, she made a dash for the waiting brougham. Courtenay thrust his stick through the window, striking Bella on the face as it drove off. Marie made the Hall in time but lost her job at 'The Empire' where the manager was afraid that Courtenay would return to make more public scenes.

Finished for the night, Marie and Bella ended up at the pub she had bought for her family in Wardour Street, 'The Prince's Tavern'. Courtenay was there, waiting for her, and shouted 'I am going to ... well murder you tonight. I will shoot you stone dead and you will never go on stage any more.' While Marie's uncle held him, Marie and Bella fled again.

Just as she was to do with her third husband, Marie issued a warrant against Courtenay saying she went in fear of her life. On 4 June, Courtenay claimed she assaulted him with a horsewhip. Marie said that *if* she had done such a thing, it was self-defence.

A few days later Courtenay was charged at Marlborough Police Court, but as Marie was in Dublin a statement was read by her solicitor saying that she did not wish to press the charges and only desired 'that her husband should be made to find sureties to keep the peace towards her'. Courtenay refused and the case came up when Marie returned.

Courtenay's solicitor gave the other side of the story, claiming that Courtenay had only gone to the theatre to 'remonstrate' with Marie about 'certain persons that would be made co-respondents in the Divorce Court'. He denied that Courtenay threatened her and said the whole point was whether Marie went in fear of her husband, and claimed she did not. But the Magistrate summed up against him and ordered Courtenay to find two sureties of £50 each to keep the peace for six months and to enter the sum of £100 with the alternative of a month's imprisonment.

The marriage was finished after seven years and Courtenay vanished from the scene. He was a weak, difficult man and was maddened at seeing her hand-out a small fortune to strangers rather than himself, especially when he lost at the races. He must have felt an alien in his own house occupied by her family and friends. Above all there was the tension between a young wife flushed with success and a husband who was a failure.

While her career prospered, her marriage suffered. Seldom do private and professional happiness soar together and the particular, and peculiar demands of a life on the Halls made any regular domestic life impossible. Frequent tours of the provinces, travelling on Sundays, meant long absences from home. Even when she was in London, like her year's engagement at 'The Oxford' in 1891, she found it difficult to return before midnight. The journey back to Lewisham by horse was a long one.

Percy Courtenay was the first to pay the penalty for being 'Mister Lloyd'.

10 The Magic of Marie

For the three winters of 1891–93 Marie played in Pantomime at Drury Lane, from Boxing Day to March. This was an accolade, but Marie pretended to be unimpressed when the impressario Augustus Harris asked her to lunch.

'What theatre did you say?' she asked innocently.

'Drury Lane,' boomed Harris.

'But I've been playing the Old Mo in Drury Lane already, do you want me to go back?'

'I mean *the* Drury Lane Theatre, the Royal Theatre.'

'Where's that?'

'My dear young lady, you must have seen the sentries outside.'

'Oh! Do you mean that horrible-looking place which stands at the end of the Lane with the soldiers round it? Why, I always thought that place was the prison! Still, I'll go there if you pay me enough.'

This is the sort of story that sounds too tiresome to be true. Marie admitted to a friend that when she received the invitation she felt 'the proudest little woman in the world'.

At the age of twenty-one she joined the 'brilliant band of Old Drury': Dan Leno, Herbert Campbell and Little Tich. She played Princess Allfair in *Humpty-Dumpty* in 1891, Red Riding Hood in *Little Bo Peep* in 1892, and Polly in *Robinson Crusoe* in 1893. This gave her prestige, but she was never completely at ease in the special atmosphere of Pantomime. It was too restricted for her and once when she improvised, she almost got the sack. She was in her grandmother's cottage in Red Riding Hood and Harris thought it would be a nice touch if she said her prayers before going to bed. Marie did this obediently, knelt by the bed and clasped her hands, until she heard Dan Leno give a deafening stage whisper from the wings 'Marie, look under the bed.'

This was all she needed. She looked under the bed and unable to find *it* began a search of the entire room while the audience roared with laughter. But Harris was not amused and made her promise not to do anything like it again.

The critics were reserved. William Archer admitted that the scene in which she 'disrobed' was 'the most successful incident of the evening . . . At every string she untied, the gallery gave a gasp of satisfaction; and when Mr Dan Leno exhibited himself in a red flannel petticoat and pair of stays, the whole house literally yelled with delight', except for Archer. 'You may think it odd, and even un-gallant, but somehow I don't seem to yearn for the privilege of assisting at Miss Marie Lloyd's toilet, or admiring Mr Dan Leno in deshabillé; but amid all that vast audience, I was evidently in a minority of one.'

Marie was too individual for the teamwork of a Pantomime; nor was she successful in her one attempt at revue in a show called *The Revue* at 'The Tivoli' with Little Tich in 1902; nor in a play especially written for her by the dramatic critic Chance Newton called *The A.B.C. Girl* or *Flossie the Frivolous*. This opened in Wolverhampton but never reached London. As Marie said of one of her performances at 'The Lane' – 'It was bloody awful, eh?'

Her sense of fun was meant for Music Hall alone and now she returned to it. As soon as Robinson Crusoe, and the Court Case were over, she made a brief tour of Halls in the provinces and left for New York on 29 August, where she appeared at 'The Imperial Theatre'. This was the second of several visits across the Atlantic.

She returned to England in November after a rough crossing on The Umbria, and was greeted with a roar of applause when she came on stage. A critic wrote: 'The audience soon found the popular little lady had lost none of the brightness and chic that are her principal passports to public appreciation.'

She took a whole page in *The Music Hall and Theatre Review* proclaiming her return:

Miss Marie Lloyd, *THE* London Favourite, has returned to town after a triumphant Tour of seven months' duration. She will now fulfil a series of engagements at the leading London Halls extend-ing over two years – Palace, Shaftesbury Avenue, London; Shore-ditch; every evening. Brilliant Repertory! Charming Dresses!!

Unique Personality ! ! ! Christmas, 'Dick Whittington', Crown Theatre, Peckham. Agent George Ware.

Typically immodest, but these were years of success and she worked hard for her popularity. Sometimes she'd play three of the leading Syndicate Halls in one night : 'The Oxford' at 9.40; the 'Pavilion' 10.10; and the 'Tivoli' 10.35 – with hardly a minute's rest in between. Admirers used to follow her from one hall to another.

At the London 'Pavilion' in 1895 she was billed as a 'Comedienne', but the billing varied. At 'The Empire' 1892 it was 'serio', and in 1893 'Serio-comic'. At 'The Alhambra' she graduated to 'Popular Serio-comic'. At 'The Oxford' she varied between 'The Droll, The Oxford Favourite' in 1892, to 'Comedienne' 1893, and back to 'Droll' in 1894. In 1895 she was plain 'Comedienne' again.

In 1902, heading a gala anniversary bill at 'The Middlesex' in Drury Lane, she was presented as : ' "Our Marie" The Popular and Only Marie Lloyd.'

Her fame was international. She topped the bill above all other continental stars at the Winter Gardens in Berlin and was received in Paris (1893) with greater acclaim than any English comedienne who had preceded her. Several of her songs had a French flavour – *The Naughty Continong* – *Twiggy Vous* – *I'm Just Back from Paris* – and *The Coster Honeymoon in Paris*. Of the few recordings that survive, *The Coster Girl in Paris* (which may be an alternative title for both *The Coster Honeymoon* ... and *I'm Just Back* ...) conveys her jauntiness best of all – that 'friendly, assured impertinence of her voice' as Colin Macinnes describes it :

> Seen the twinkle in me eye?
> Just come back from France, that's why –
> Me and Bill went over there to spend our 'oneymoon.
> First time I'd been in foreign parts,
> Did I like it? Bless your hearts!
> Can't say any more than that it ended up too soon.
> But don't think I've done with good old England – not likely.
> Born and bred down 'Ackney Road, ah! an' proud to own it too.
> You like me make up?
> Ain't it great?

MARIE LLOYD
and Music Hall

The latest thing from Paris – straight!
Gives a girl a chance to show what she can do!
And I'd like to go again
To Paris on the Seine,
For Paris is a proper pantomime,
And if they'd only shift the 'Ackney Road and plant it over
      there,
I'd like to live in Paris all the time.

A typical Marie Lloyd song in which she confides to the audience – 'Like me make up?' and rejoices in the glamour of foreign parts, but shows that her heart belongs to 'Ackney.

The story is told of Marie found sobbing in her dressing-room after her first appearance in Paris, refusing to go on stage again – 'Take me back to where they love me, away from these hateful people.'

'What is the matter?' asked the friend, genuinely astonished after the wonderful reception she'd received.

'I've done my best and they call me a beast.'

He explained that the shouts of 'Bis, Bis' were cries for 'more' and Marie was mollified. I give this story for what it's worth.

On her third visit to New York, with Alec Hurley, the Americans liked her more than she liked them. She gave a party at The Astor Hotel to celebrate King Edward vII's birthday, with a Union Jack as the table-cloth and decorations in red, white and blue. She hired a band and led the other British artists in *God Save the King*, determined to show the Americans that her heart still lay in 'Ackney. But on the last night at 'The Colonial Music Hall', she was given a presentation on behalf of her American colleagues with the generous statement: 'To Marie Lloyd, the greatest artiste and best friend that we have ever known.'

What *was* so special about her?

People ask this as if there might be a single answer – but of course there isn't. But there are clues. Though the recordings left to us are thin, they are totally distinctive with that characteristic catch in her voice. Her delivery is precise and determined and she gives the impression of knowing exactly what she is doing. There is no stage cockney drawl, like we have today; the emphasis is clipped. Daisy Wood said that 'Marie never had what you could call a good voice. When she sang a song, she was in it. She got into the words. She was

A rare photo of three generations—Mrs. Wood, Marie and Marie Junior.

This Lloyd family group shows (top row): Daisy, Rosie, John, Grace and Alice; (middle row): Father, Mother, Marie; (bottom row): Annie, Maud and Sydney.

Marie goes for a car ride, accompanied by three smiling sisters.

A photograph taken in 1901 in Adelaide, Australia. Left to right: Ted Hanley, Annie Wood, Marie Lloyd and Alec Hurley.

'I Ain't Nobody In Perticuler.' Alec Hurley's portrait appears on the sheet music cover.

(Left) *Bernard Dillon as a successful jockey.* (Below) *Marie relaxes in a hammock.*

(Above) *In this race, Bernard Dillon is on the left, nearest the camera.* (Left) *A wedding group. Bernard Dillon as best man at the marriage of Marie's niece to Joe Mott.*

the character. And every word you could hear.' The recordings bear this out.

The few flickering seconds of film that exist, hint of her vitality as she runs on and off stage. Another glimpse, at the costumiers, when she was much older, suggests the clowning of a natural comic, though the smile was probably as determined then as her delivery.

What *was* she like? From this distance it's only possible to imagine. I suspect that the single characteristic that explained her appeal, was a sense of *fun*. Wonderfully infectious. As soon as her number came up in lights on the side of the stage and her bright intro music was played, I bet that people were smiling, even chuckling, before she ever appeared.

Until the two masterpieces at the end – *Don't Dilly Dally* and *Cromwell*, many of her songs were terrible – but it's obvious that her fun carried them through. Sometimes she'd sing one of her cockney numbers wearing one of her grandest dresses, to make them all the funnier:

> We went gathering carslips
> Moo-cow came to me
> Wagged 'is apparatus
> And I said unto he –
> Rumptiddly – umptiddley – umptiddely – ay
> Our little lot so gay – we don't care what we do or what we
>   say

She *must* have done miracles with such lyrics. She sang these as a cockney child (according to Mary Howard who was told this by her mother), one of a gang out in the country for the day, frightened of cows, making blue jokes about cow-pats and all the while she wore a beautiful hostess gown, wiping her nose on her sleeve, kicking up her legs, hat slipping back. She could change in a second from a great lady to a gutter snipe.

She had a nice sense of mockery, imitating upper-class women in tiny, illuminating flashes – 'Ah, Lady What's-her-name, how *nice* to see you . . .' in a monologue called 'Lady Jane'.

She retained a simplicity on stage, just as she did off it. The audience knew that she treated fame with contempt and never indulged in airs or graces. Her tastes were basic, champagne at

Romano's or more likely winkles from the stall. She loved kippers and shocked one lodging house by insisting on having them for lunch and she got them. She went to Sheekey's off St Martin's Lane for jellied eels and a stage-hand at the Hackney Empire remembers how she asked him who sold the best stewed eels in the neighbourhood and asked him to get her two shilling's worth every night after the show – 'Be a pal jack and don't forget my eels'. She loved winkles and listened for the sound of the winkle man coming down the road with his cart and bell; as soon as she heard him, the maid was sent out with a bowl.

In such ways she had direct contact with the audience, and shared her own enjoyments and experiences with them, unlike Vesta Tilley who was aloof by comparison.

She was gay in the glorious sense of the word, before it became debased. But underlining the gaiety was an understanding of the problems and disasters the audience knew too well. What could be more poignant than the opening lines, by Fred Leigh, of *Don't Dilly Dally*?

> We had to move away
> 'Cos the rent we couldn't pay,
> The moving van came round just after dark;
> There was me and my old man
> Shoving things inside the van,
> Which we'd often done before, let me remark . . .

Stopping at too many pubs, she forgot the new address and told the audience of her distress, but went on to treat it with hilarious resignation, bred from familiarity – confidingly, she admitted:

> Oh I'm in such a mess, I don't know the new address
> I don't even know the blessed neighbourhood
> And I feel as if I might
> Have to stop out all the night
> And that ain't going to do me any good.
> I don't make no complaint, but I'm coming over faint
> What I want now is a good substantial feed
> And I sorta, kinda feel, if I don't soon have a meal
> I shall have to rob the linnet of his seed.

My old man said follow the van
And don't dilly dally on the way
Off went the cart with me home packed in it
I followed on with my old cock linnet
I dillied, I dallied, I dallied and I dillied
I lost me way and don't know where to roam
Who's going to put up the old iron bedstead
If I can't find my way home?

We still sing the rollicking chorus today but the words no longer
have meaning for us. Think of the association then.

The same with the brilliant lyrics of 'It's a bit of a ruin that
Cromwell knocked about a bit' in which she gets drunk, again, and
her handbag is robbed while she's sitting in the long grass with a
stranger – the story is slightly desperate, but this is counteracted by
the music which is indomitably cheerful :

It's a bit of a ruin that Cromwell knocked about a bit,
One that Oliver Cromwell knocked about a bit.
In the gay old days there used to be some doings
No wonder that the poor old Abbey went to ruins.
Those who've studied history sing and shout of it
And you can bet your life there isn't a doubt of it
Outside the Oliver Cromwell last Saturday night
I was one of the ruins that Cromwell knocked about a bit.

Some of the finest songs of Music Hall had this indomitable quality
of cocking a snoop at misfortune. Vesta Victoria's *Waiting at the
Church* – 'Lord how it did upset me' – with lyrics by Fred Leigh, one
of the best and most prolific of the writers; Gus Elan's *It's a great
big shame*; and Lily Morris' plaintive cry *Why am I always the
Bridesmaid, never the blushing bride*?

The Londoners with their unique sense of humour, loved this
defiance of disaster. Marie recognized this with her comment on
Dan Leno, as great a comic as she was a comedienne.

'Ever seen his eyes?' she asked. 'The saddest eyes in the whole
world. That's why we all laughed at Danny. Because if we hadn't
laughed, we should have cried ourselves sick. I believe that's what
real comedy is, you know. It's almost like crying . . .'

What *was* she like? The comments of people who saw Marie at her best convey a glimmering of the magic. James Agate attempted the answer: '. . . the time will come when she will be a thing of the past, old dear (a reference to one of her songs) the old words but with a tragic difference. What, then will remain? A few faded photographs and a few records stored away . . . What was she like? Our grandchildren will doubtless be told that she was a vulgar singer of indecent songs whereby she will be confounded in the general mind with the big-bosomed broad-buttocked, butcher-thighed Principal Boys . . . Now though Marie filled every corner of the stage, she was a little woman poised upon tiny elegant feet. She was chic in the way Rejane was chic. If Sans-Gene was the mirror of an Empire, Marie was the looking glass of the Promenade. Whatever she wore took on the gleam of white satin . . .'

The critic of *The Era* noticed the clever habit of delaying her entrance 'with the conspicuous success that she always creates'.

This deliberate titillation of the audience was one of her trademarks. Her breezy intro music was played and then repeated to create the maximum suspense, and when she finally deigned to appear she stood there in the spotlight almost staring the audience out, and then she'd start her song conversationally as if she was telling a story. 'She always took her audience into her confidence,' said her sister Anne.

Don Ross, the last impressario of Music Hall, described the atmosphere of her entrance: 'Marie's number goes up at either side of the proscenium, immediately there is a hum of excitement, a chuckle of merriment, and her music starts. And so, as the excitement grew, up would swing the house-tabs on to a full stage, possibly a Palace set or a drawing-room set and up on the right hand corner the limes were all focused and then – a moment of sheer magic – she would appear.

'Always with a lovely smile, looking full of good humour and almost saying with her expression "Now we're going to have some fun", she would walk with a nice, brisk swinging gait down to the footlights.

'She would be wearing a beautiful gown, very elegant, possibly black-sequined or a moonlight blue, figure fitting, and on her head a very smart little hat, as like as not bursting with ospreys or paradise plumes at just the right angle.

'And so she would come down to the footlights and stand smiling

at the applause. Hanging on a ribbon, she had diamond lorgnettes and
as the orchestra kept playing the ad lib "dummety dum te dummety
dum', Marie would raise them to her eyes and look round the
audience.'

Sometimes, as she stood there, a cry would come from the gallery
– 'Give us a dirty look Marie!'

'No need to, you've already got one.'

Such patter, was part of her act. One story describes her arriving
with an umbrella, waving it in front of her to the point of embarrassment until it opened – 'Thank god! I haven't had it up for months!'

Another time she made a production of picking a banana skin off
the stage – with the aside to the audience – 'If the man who threw
this wants to get his skin back, he can come to my dressing-room
afterwards.'

And when she was late, there was the famous excuse – 'Sorry I'm
late, I got blocked in the Strand.'

Several admirers refer to her timing. When she was only twenty-
two, Bernard Shaw said – 'She has an exceptionally quick ear for
both pitch and rhythm ... the intonation and lilt of her songs are
perfect.' Max Beerbohm, who included her with Queen Victoria
and Florence Nightingale as the three most memorable women of
the age, said: 'She had an exquisitely sensitive ear, impeccable
phrasing and timing. But sheer joy of living was always her strongest
point.'

The Dowager Lady Aberconway has written to me – 'My
memory of her is that she had more stage sense – (how to *fill* the
stage, *keep* tension going) than anyone I saw, and her timing was
magnetic – I can use no other word. Her cockney songs were great
works of art.'

'As an artist she was very relaxed' wrote Don Ross, 'she moved
very little but when she did move, even if it were only a movement
of the hand, it meant something.

'On the repeat choruses of her smart songs she did a little movement with her feet and a turn or two, clean cut and neat, like everything about her.'

'Relaxed' – 'Placid' – what an effort this façade must have cost
her. Charlie Chaplin, who worked on the same bill when he was a boy,
has described how he 'would watch her wide-eyed, this anxious,
plump little lady pacing nervously up and down behind the scenes,

irritable and apprehensive until the moment came for her to go on. Then she was immediately gay and relaxed.'

Like all the Lloyd sisters she had tiny, delicate features. James Agate, said that 'Her "dial", as the Cockney would put it, was the most expressive on the halls. She had beautiful hands and feet. She knew every board on the stage and every inch of every board, and in the perfection of her technical accomplishment rivalled her great contemporary of another world, Mrs Kendall. Briefly – she knew her business.'

The Era's critic, in 1894, also referred to her 'chic'. Her appearance on stage was a vital part of her performance. She was billed as appearing with 'New Songs and Paris Gowns'.

Marie designed many of the dresses herself, and her hard-working mother and an aunt made them in a special upstairs room in her house. A journalist described Mrs Wood's favourite – short in the waist, low in the neck, with straps instead of sleeves. It was decorated with 'glittering paillettes which flashed and seemed to merge by turns in reflections of every colour imaginable. A piquant, tri-cornered hat with nodding black plumes surmounted this costume which was effectively lined with pink.'

It must have flattered the East End audiences that one of them could appear looking like a Queen. By any standard, her dresses were sumptuous. Usually she changed during her act, and as every dress, hat and accessory had a separate box, Marie went on tour with a safari of luggage. Accessories included a long string of pearls, which she rubbed provocatively across her teeth.

The costumes were the work of a perfectionist. An Empire Dress was 'a mass of exquisite embroidery, a pattern of wild blush roses carried out in silks, sequins, spangles, and gold and silver threads on a white satin background, while delicately tinted little shells were interwoven in a marvellous manner'. The workmanship was too fine to be properly appreciated on the stage, even from the stalls.

Even in her 'character' songs, every detail was correct. In *My Old Man*, no shiny shoes peeped from under the worn-out dress and shawl. On her head she wore a black straw boater, favourite with the coster women of the period, and she carried the bird-cage in her hand. I've seen the original, so different from the ornate replicas artists use today. Small and rough, knocked up by the stage-carpenter, disarming in its simplicity. When she rummaged through her hand-bag in *'It's a Bit of a Ruin that Cromwell Knocked About a Bit'*, the

handbag would be old and knocked about itself; everything in it
would be right.

T. S. Eliot was one of many, unexpected admirers. He could hardly
have given her higher praise: 'In the details of her acting, Marie
Lloyd was perhaps the most perfect, in her own style, of British
actresses.' He noticed the unique relationship between Marie and
the audience:

'The attitude of audiences towards Marie Lloyd was different from
their attitude towards any other of their favourites of the day, and in
this represents the difference in her act. Marie Lloyd's audiences were
invariably sympathetic and it was through this sympathy that she
controlled them.

'I have seen Nellie Wallace interrupted by jeering or hostile comment from a boxful of East-enders; I have seen her, hardly pausing
in her act, make some quick retort that silenced her tormentors for
the rest of the evening. But I have never known Marie Lloyd to be
confronted by this kind of hostility; in any case, the feelings of the
vast majority of the audience were so manifestly on her side that no
objector would have dared lift his voice ... no other comedian succeeded so well in giving expression to the life of the audience, in
raising it to a kind of art. It was, I think, this capacity for expressing
the soul of the people that made Marie Lloyd unique and that made
her audience, even when they joined in the chorus, not so much
hilarious as happy.'

Those last few words convey much of the magic of Marie. And
there was something more – that *wink* – 'the most incredible wink'.
'With her famous wink', wrote Don Ross, 'timed to the fraction of a
second, she could make an apparently simple remark very much more.
As with Max Miller in later years, so with Marie in her time, almost
anything she said was pounced on by the audience as meaning more
than the spoken word.'

And *that* was the cause of the trouble!

11 The Ladies of the Empire

Was Marie Lloyd offensive? – No.

Was she dirty? – Probably.

Was she vulgar? – Undeniably!

The business with the banana and the umbrella show how far she could go – *if* the stories are true. I heard them from an old docker in a Swansea pub and a BBC producer respectively, but just as most dirty stories are supposed to originate from the Stock Exchange today, any dirty crack then was attributed to Marie.

But many of the stories *are* true. Marie loved to shock, especially when someone was starchy. A much-loved, but naïve singer once shared a dressing-room with her. They seldom appeared on the same bill, for both were 'headliners' but this was a charity benefit.

'Have a drink' was Marie's greeting. The artist refused primly and Marie, with a muttered 'Too bloody pure to live', downed the glass herself. Then she produced a really filthy chamber pot that she carried around with her, for she was too big a star to share the communal lavatory, and used it, stark naked. 'As an artist, yes' said the shattered singer afterwards, 'but as a person, never mention her name to me again.'

She made a point of teasing Ada Reeve, who was also rather proper. Sailing into Romano's one lunchtime, Marie spotted her in a corner sitting with an important Manager. 'That's a nice bit of cock you've got there!' she cried out pleasantly as she passed them.

On stage, it wasn't so much what she said but the way she said it or rather sang it – for the songs were under constant attack. But on this charge, James Agate defended her: 'Her genius consisted in the skill and emphasis with which she drove home the offensive point. She employed a whole armoury of shrugs and leers, and to reveal every cranny of the mind utilized each articulation of the body. No one was ever worse for her performance. Everything depends, surely, upon what these squeamish critics mean by offensive and "worse".

It will not be claimed, I think, that *A little of What you Fancy Does you Good* turned the young men out of the heated Music Hall into the Strand determined to look neither to the right nor to the left.

'. . . she preached the world and the flesh, and glorified in their being the very devil. None ever left the theatre feeling spiritually better. From that blight, at least they were free.

'There was nothing sad or secret about this idol. She knew that the great English public will open its arms to vice, provided it is presented as a frolic.

'. . . Yvette Guilbert harrowed the soul with the pathos of her street-walkers; Marie Lloyd had intense delight in her draggle-tails. She showed them in their splendour, not in their misery . . .

'Again she proved herself an infinitely greater realist than others more highly esteemed. She depicted the delights of humble life, the infinite joy of mean streets . . . Was Marie Lloyd vulgar? Undoubtedly. That great quality was her chief glory. She relished and expounded those things she knew to be dear to the common heart.'

Marie conducted her own defence, with her usual lack of tact, when she returned to New York in 1897. Her scandalous reputation had travelled before her. 'I might as well say right here that my songs are not blue – at least not half as blue as they are painted. Just because I sing them, they are suggestive and vulgar and nasty and everything else your cheap little reporters can think to call them. I'll bet if I sang the songs of Solomon set to music I would be accused of making them bad, just because people at the halls want songs that are not quite dead marches and I give it to them. You take the pit on a Saturday night or a Bank Holiday. You don't suppose they want Sunday school stuff do you? They want lively stuff with music they can learn quickly. Why, if I was to try to sing highly moral songs they would fire ginger-beer bottles and beer mugs at me. They don't pay their sixpences and shillings at a Music Hall to hear the Salvation Army.

'But mind you, I don't say that my songs are thick simply because they are lively. The trouble is that people are looking for blue, and I can't help it, you know, if they want to turn and twist my meanings.'

Vigorously and none too convincingly, she defended specific songs like *Saturday to Monday*. 'A "Johnny" asks a chorus girl to go on a little yachting trip with him. It's all right. He's got a chaperone aboard and fizz and stuff, yet because I sing it it must be bad and everybody pretends it's thick and musty. It's not half as bad as lots of songs other people sing. The words are absolutely clean :

> Oh, will you come with me
> To Brighton-by-the-sea
> And you will go upon my yacht on Sunday?
> If you'll only say the word,
> I'll take you like a bird,
> And bring you safely back to town on Monday.

Can you see where the thickness comes in? Why, even a parson couldn't see it was blue unless someone told him.

'It's just the same with the Railroad song. It's not at all thick, and yet the people get clever and say it means all sorts of things. I can't help that, can I? I can't make people think straight.

'People are awful queer, and I don't see the use of trying to please them.'

She concluded – 'You Americans are awfully clever, but you are too smart here, for you find things blue and thick that an Eton boy could hear without being hurt by. And I guess I don't hurt the Music Hall audiences much, even if they do see a whole lot in my songs that isn't there.'

She protested too much! Numbers like *The Railroad Song*, also known as 'The Girl who'd never had her ticket punched before', were plainly intended for their double meaning. As the title of another of her favourites suggested – 'Every little gesture has a meaning of its own.'

Even if the audiences did read too much into the songs, Marie rapidly acquired the reputation of a scandalous woman, even a sexsymbol of her time. Nice, middle-class families forbade their children to see her. But as I have said, Marie was blamed for the bad reputation of Music Hall itself.

From the outside, many of the halls were as opulent as the names suggest – 'Alhambra', 'Empire', 'Palace' and 'Pavilion'. And it wasn't just the London 'Pavilion', which claimed to be the first 'Music Hall de Luxe', but also the 'Pavilion' down in Whitechapel. When this was re-built it held more people than Covent Garden, had a 70ft stage only exceeded by La Scala in Milan, and a vast chandelier with 300 lights which reflected into thousands when it was lit.

But behind the elegant façades, the roots of Music Hall were firmly

down to earth and to many people they only concealed a hell within.
They were condemned, like the Penny Gaff in its time, not only for
the depravity of the entertainment but even more for the depraved
people they attracted.

Certainly there was a rowdiness. Two newspaper reports hint at
the type of trouble managers had to contend with. On 12 November
1887, a boy of fourteen struck a checktaker with a ginger-beer bottle
at Sanger's Amphitheatre. The magistrate sent him to a Naval Training school in Cornwall – 'we shall see if you will not turn out a
bright sailor and be a credit to your country'. This offence was
harmless enough, but such attacks were so common that waiters often
had their bottles chained to the trays, as they served drink in the
auditorium, and orchestras were protected with iron grilles.

A more vicious form of violence was the blackmailing of artists
by layabouts who hung around the stage door and promised wild
applause if they were paid. The threat was implicit, that if they did
not get the money there'd be a hostile demonstration instead with
boos and catcalls. One victim was the male impersonator Millie
Hylton who was attacked after the performance when she was walking home with her brother. Artists were reluctant to give evidence,
because managers disliked trouble, and she claimed she must have
been mistaken for someone else. On 10 March 1888, George Harris,
24, was sentenced to a month's hard labour for 'demanding money
as a bribe for applause' outside 'The Canterbury'.

Apart from rowdiness and blackmail, there were charges of
drunkenness and obscenity – but the greatest offence of all was the
open prostitution. Undeniably, the promenades did provide a perfect
pitch for the prostitutes. What really shocked the establishment was
the way these women fitted in so elegantly – they didn't *look* guilty!

Writing in 1870, Daniel Kirwan the American observer, claimed
that 'if the "Alhambra" and every Music Hall hell like it in London
were suddenly scorched up by fire from heaven, it would be the most
incomparable benefit ever bestowed upon the English metropolis,
and a saving grace to thousands of young English men and women –
both in body and soul. And the reason for this is that women are
allowed admission at the payment of a price, without the escort of a
man.

'And are these women calculated, by their manner, dress or
appearance to shock or warn people by their degradation? On the
contrary, they are cheerful, pleasant looking girls, of quite fair

breeding, and of a far better taste in their dress than the honest wives and sweethearts of the mechanics and shopkeepers, who sit in the place of virtue, within the painted railing.'

Twenty years later when Marie entered the battle it was the Ladies of 'The Empire' who gave offence – the glamorous courtesans who paraded up and down the promenade of the Music Hall in Leicester Square. They sound magnificent. Their arrogance, with not a trace of wretchedness, incensed the middle-class.

Macqueen Pope describes them as: '. . . the aristocrats of their "profession". Amazing creatures, amazingly dressed, of all races and speech . . . they moved quietly and slowly, to and fro, with a rather feline grace. A tiger pacing in its cage has such a gift of movement. They were quite unmistakable, yet their manners were excellent. They never accosted a man, at the most he might feel the soft touch of a hand against him or the faint pressure of a silk clad body if he stood watching the show.

'There was never any loud chatter, shrieking laughter or bad language. One complaint to the management and they were barred. And that was that, for them, tragedy, irrevocable loss of prestige and descent to the depths.

'There were all types for all tastes, from the regally majestic, to the quiet and demure; from the bold, flashing merry eye to the modestly downcast eyelid. But there was allure everywhere.'

Willson Disher was another visitor who found it inoffensive, enjoying the charm of the place and the 'mellow Victorians who exchanged memories and were glad to find you listening.

'Outcries against the vice of the promenade seemed justified only when I became aware one night that a young French woman next to me in the crush round the bar, had left off her corsets. All this suggests now is that she had anticipated the general fashion by a few years. Then it was scandalous behaviour.'

The 'Empire' was luxurious with deep pile carpets and footmen in blue and gold livery. It advertised itself on a programme as 'The Cosmopolitan Club of the World' and when an Englishman arrived back from some far-flung corner of the Empire he headed straight to the other 'Empire' of Leicester Square.

Great care was taken to avoid trouble. On Boat Race night, the rowdiest in the year, they cleared the tables of bottles, glasses and anything breakable. Bodyguards were stationed all round the Hall and the Manager wearing full evening dress and white kid gloves would go up to any young man causing trouble and pat him politely on the shoulder; then he'd be thrown out. Concealed in the Manager's white glove was a piece of chalk which left its warning mark and if the young man staggered round to another entrance he was recognized as a trouble-maker and thrown out again.

Everyone entering 'The Empire' had to stand the scrutiny of four men; soliciting was condemned. But in spite of all these precautions, 'The Empire' and its Promenade were anathema to a large number of people – foremost of these was a formidable woman with the imposing name of Mrs Ormiston Chant.

12 Winston Churchill versus Mrs Chant

Mrs Chant was the Chairman of the Purity Party and an enemy of Music Hall. She claimed it 'catered for people who had a small proportion of brains'. Mrs Chant opposed the renewal of the Music Halls' licences at the Magistrates Sessions. In 1894 she summoned her supporters in the LCC to purge 'The Empire' of the Ladies of the Promenade. She was challenged by a young Army officer who came up from Sandhurst twice a month to visit this very promenade, Winston Churchill. 'We were scandalized by Mrs Chant's charges and insinuations' he wrote in *My Early Life*. 'We had never seen anything to complain of in the behaviour of either sex. Indeed the only point upon which criticism, as it seemed to us, might justly be directed was the strict and even rough manner in which the enormous uniformed commissionaires immediately removed, and even thrust forcibly into the street, anyone who had inadvertently overstepped the bounds of true temperance. We thought Mrs Chant's movement entirely uncalled for and contrary to the best traditions of British freedom. In this cause I was extremely anxious to strike a blow.'

Churchill was not alone. The *Daily Telegraph*, in an article headed 'Prudes on the Prowl', announced that someone had started a counter movement called The Entertainments Protection League. Churchill wrote in, was invited to the first meeting, and even prepared the first public speech of his career, already Churchillian – '. . . upon the inherent rights of British subjects. But when he arrived at the meeting he was the only member, apart from the Founder who complained 'I don't know what's happened to the country. They seem to have no spirit left.' Churchill pawned his gold watch and returned to Sandhurst.

Mrs Chant had greater success. A screen of canvas and trellis-work was erected between the promenade and the bars, and the prostitutes concealed discreetly. It was typical British compromise and Churchill was 'filled with scorn at its hypocrisy. I had no idea in those days of the enormous and unquestionably helpful part that humbug plays in the social life of great peoples dwelling in a state of democratic freedom.'

The following Saturday, Churchill happened to find himself at the 'Empire' with a group of young men who started poking their walking sticks through the canvas. 'Naturally I could not hang back', writes Churchill, 'suddenly a most strange thing happened. The entire crowd, numbering some two or three hundred people became excited and infuriated.' They tore the barricades down, marched around Leicester Square waving bits of the screen, and Churchill mounted the debris to make his maiden speech : 'You have seen us tear down these barricades tonight; see that you pull down those who are responsible for them at the coming election.' There was wild applause and Churchill was reminded of the taking of the Bastille.

Meanwhile the bars at 'The Empire' were closed and brass railings replaced the canvas and the trellis work.

With the British genius for turning their bigots into jokes, an effigy of Mrs Chant was burnt at the stake, as Guy Fawkes on the fifth of November. As Churchill had urged, her supporters, described as "irresponsible volunteers, amateur detectives and fussy busy-bodies', were routed in the Council elections the following March. 'The Music Hall proprietors,' wrote *The Era*, 'have a very strong ally in the public, whose opinion of the Puritan Party was expressed in no uncertain voice at the County Council elections . . .'

Mrs Chant sailed for America denying the rumour that she left London for the express purpose of being absent when the licences came up again in October. She was highly sensitive to criticism. She accused the English press of abusing her 'in every conceivable manner, almost entirely ignoring that I was but the chosen representative of others'. She made the threat that if the Council did reverse the 'sound policy' adopted in 1894, and restored 'the evils which previously existed', she would see that energetic action was taken when the licensing laws came round yet again in 1896. Her fears were realized. In October the Council reversed the closure of the 'Empire Promenade', on the curious grounds that as there had been no improvement in the character of the audience the restrictions might just as well be lifted. Strange logic. Even stranger, by one vote they refused to restore the Promenade at the 'Palace' which enjoyed a blameless reputation under Charles Morton.

MARIE LLOYD
and Music Hall

The Era pounced on the illogicality: 'more absurd contradiction could hardly have been made than the two votes which decided the fate of the two establishments. It is obvious that if it be right that the 'Empire Theatre' should have its promenade restored to it, it cannot also be right that the Palace should be denied the privilege of possessing a similar lounging place.'

They compared it to a pedagogue who says to a bad boy 'I have tried this and tried that and can do nothing with you. I give up, you can do as you like'. And says to the good boy, Morton, 'I have no fault to find therefore I shall treat you with rigorous severity.' 'If Morton wants a promenade, and other managers have a promenade, he ought to have his promenade too.'

The Era also pointed out the inconsistency in wanting the Music Hall visitor to stay in his seat all evening, while refusing 'The Palace' the right to serve drink in the auditorium. By preventing the customer from having refreshment brought to his seat, they only drove him out into the bars. This shows what an accepted part drink played in the Music Hall evening.

While *The Era* welcomed the change of the Council's policy and agreed it was becoming wiser in the light of experience, it asked for one law for all: 'The removal of the barriers and the restoration of the drinking bars to the Empire Theatre is practically a confession that the question raised by Mrs Chant and her friends is not to be settled by merely material means. Unless the Legislature is prepared to forbid fast women the use of the streets, of the theatres, and of the churches we cannot see how any important alterations can be made. To throw on the box-office keeper of any place of amusement the task of discriminating between vice and virtue in his issue of tickets would be absurd – indeed dangerous. We trust the time is not far distant when there will be one and the same rule for all the Music Halls in London.'

The Ladies of the Promenade returned to the 'Empire', with even more discretion than before, and Mrs Chant continued but to slightly less effect. 'A huge joke, a Sunday night farce, the all-pervading motive of which was self-advertisement' was how a ladies' magazine described her speech on 'The Music Hall; its use and abuse' made to the Playgoer's Club in November.

Mrs Chant put her case revealingly. Comparing the theatre to the pulpit, she claimed that Music Hall catered to people 'who out of sheer tiredness of brain or want of a superior education could hardly appreciate a play'. This was greeted with laughter and cries of 'No!' She suggested that at least half an hour of Music Hall should be devoted to scenes from some high-class novel 'calculated to elevate and instruct the minds of the audience'. Saying in effect that as they couldn't think for themselves someone else had to do it, she admitted she had no more right 'to quarrel with vulgar entertainment than with a vulgar bonnet'. She wanted people to live and be glad – but inevitably there was a *but*: 'there were evils in connection with the stage which could be, and should be got rid of.'

Surprisingly, she said that some chorus girls weren't paid at all, others hardly enough to live on, and hoped that one outcome of the agitation would be the increase of profit-sharing in the theatres as well as the factories. As a Christian moralist she did not want to abolish, but to purify art.

Charles Coborn (The Man who broke the Bank of Monte Carlo) said her campaign would do an incalculable good to Music Hall because so many people wouldn't go there because of the drawbacks she was trying to remove. Someone less sanctimonious said he didn't believe for a moment that Mrs Chant was a true lover of art but part of a sect which wanted to stop every kind of rational amusement and reduce life to their own dull standard.

In 1896, 'The Oxford' was their new target and its promenade denounced as 'a market for vice and drinking'.

A Nonconformist Minister, the Reverend La Pla of Harringay, appeared for one of the protesting Vigilance Committees. He said he came forward in the 'interests of the purity of Music Halls' after seeing the notices inviting the public to give evidence. He claimed one night he was accosted at the 'Oxford' and counted forty-eight 'gay women'. There was 'sensation in court' (literally reported in *The Era*), when he admitted that he hadn't actually talked to any of the women but assumed they were 'gay' because of their bearing.

The most accosted family in England were the Reeds. Miss Carina Reed, opposed the *entire* renewal of the licence, and objected to a certain dance.

Counsel: What was there objectionable in the dance?

Miss Reed: The man disguised as a female had very scanty clothing and the attitudes he assumed were very improper. One of the men threw 'the woman' over his shoulder, and in that process 'she' was entirely exposed. Afterwards I found the woman was not a woman,

5—MLATMH * *

but a man in disguise, because they came in afterwards with their wigs off.

Miss Reed had been to the 'Oxford' eight times in the last few months and heard women bargaining with men for money – 'I heard her say, "Come and give me two pounds".'

Sir J. P. Maple, a member of the committee, suggested she might have been trying to borrow it.

Cross-examined, Miss Reed admitted she went to the Halls to look for something wrong.

Mr Gill : Have you ever been turned out of these places?

Miss Reed : Yes.

Mr Gill : For accosting a man?

Miss Reed : No. The manager turned me out.

Mr Gill : He said you were accosting a man?

Miss Reed : He said I looked at a man.

Mr Reed (I assume this was her father) followed her to say that he too had been accosted by a girl who asked if it was the end of the programme – 'There was nothing in the words. It was not exactly what she said but the way she said it.'

Mr Gill : Have you much spare time for looking after the morals of other people?

Mr Reed : No, I did it at personal inconvenience.

Mr Gill : Who selected you as a suitable person to judge of morals and taste?

Mr Reed : I was not selected, I offered to go.

Finally, Mrs Reed (presumably the mother) described the horrible moment when she too was accosted, by an elderly man who leant against her and asked why she didn't look more cheerful.

Terrified, Mrs Reed said she had an appointment but the man returned saying 'He has not come; he's a blackguard. Won't you come and have a drink with me?' Mrs Reed didn't answer, and left.

Mr Gill : Why did you leave your husband? Did you expect to be accosted?

Mrs Reed : I don't know why, I wanted to walk a little while.

Mr Gill : Did you see your husband accosted?

Mrs Reed : Yes; a woman went and looked in his face.

Mr Gill : What did she do then?

Mrs Reed : She smiled.

When Miss Reed was caught spying at 'The Empire', the manager turned the tables nicely and accused her of trying to attract men by getting them to speak to her. When he asked her to sit down she refused, so he gave her money back and told her to leave. Now the Reeds attempted their revenge. They complained of a number of songs including *Johnny Jones* which was sung by Marie Lloyd as a schoolgirl. Mrs Reed claimed it had 'an evil tendency'.

Asked if the audience took it that way, she said it encouraged the women to look at the men.

'More than they did before?'

'Yes. They laughed very much.'

'Then they didn't seem to disapprove of it?'

'No, they laughed very much. But then I saw men and women accosting one another and go off together.' Marie stood accused for encouraging the vices of the promenade – through laughter.

Admittedly there *was* a childish preoccupation with so-called 'private parts'. A singer called Lady Mansel was in trouble with a song about a girl who wandered into a man's bathing tent by mistake – 'And what I saw I must not tell you now.' Madge Ellis appeared as a schoolgirl with socks and bare legs and Mr Reed complained 'There was an objectionable raising of the skirts when a boy showed his bruise, and she replied "If you show me yours fust, I'll show you mine" '.

Marie's *Johnny Jones* was in the same tradition.

> What's that for Eh? Oh tell me Ma!
> If you won't tell me me, I'll ask Pa!
> But Ma said, 'Oh it's nothing, shut your row!'
> Well – I've asked Johnny Jones, see,
> So I know now.

Marie came on dressed as a schoolgirl, and Mrs Reed was particularly upset by one verse in the song which referred to some baby-clothes that were being knitted. Marie must have endowed the words with extraordinary suggestion as she bowled her hoop or sucked her thumb, for the words seem innocuous:

> Ah! I know something no one knows
> Ma's making oh! such pretty clothes,
> Too large for dolly, they must be –
> I'm sure they're much too small for me.
> There's little frocks and socks and shoes

MARIE LLOYD
and Music Hall

> And ribbons – reds, and pinks, and blues,
> And little bibs, as well there are
> And other things – so I asked Ma.

One evening, when Marie was appearing at 'The Empire', she heard a cry from the stalls of – 'Stop! Stop! Stop!' The orchestra squealed to a halt and Marie, afraid that someone had died in the audience, asked what had happened. Mrs Chant had happened — making her public protest against Marie Lloyd.

This was the start of the famous confrontation between Marie and the Licensing Authorities. It is legendary, but something of the sort plainly happened around this time. (Marie Lloyd Junior described such an incident to me in detail, adding: 'her songs would seem like bloody hymns today!')

I suspect the offending song was *Johnny Jones* though legend suggests it was about the girl who 'Sits among the lettuces and peas'. There's a difference of opinion on this – her sister Anne denies she ever sang such a song: 'No, she never had a song with those lines in it. That is an old story that has gone for years.' Macqueen Pope agreed: 'She is reputed to have sung a song about a market garden and its contents – nobody has yet been found who heard her do so.' But Ernest Short in *Fifty Years of Vaudeville* says 'Marie came into collision with the licensing authorities over a certain song, about a young lady who had a garden. Objection was taken to a phrase and Marie altered it.' Naomi Jacob goes further and says it was Sir Henry Tozer of the 'Tivoli' who made Marie promise to change it which she did, obediently – to 'sits among the cabbages and leeks.'

In 1964, when I advertised in *The Sunday Times* for information about Marie, I heard from an elderly woman in Brighton, and see no reason for disbelieving her.

'. . . in those carefree days before the First World War, my fiancé (later killed 1917) took me to the Oxford Music Hall (I think it was called) situated on the left-hand side going down Oxford Street, just before Tottenham Court Road.

'Marie Lloyd was one of the turns. Just before she had been taken to task by the censor for singing a song in which she had gone into the garden and "pea'd".

'I was very young and in love – was new to London and had never seen Marie Lloyd before, so that when she sang that she had gone into the garden and "leeked" I thought the applause was wonderful and joined in.

'She was so vital, so gay, even if vulgar, and of course being young (now 70 odd) I knew nothing of her wretched private life until years after. Then I wondered how she could have been so gay, so radiant.'

Whatever the song Marie appeared before the Committee. Though she was seething inwardly, she sang the songs straight without a flicker of expression. The effect could hardly have been more innocuous and the committee were stunned by such apparent innocence after expecting something obscene. After a brief consultation they had to tell her they could find nothing offensive and she could go.

It was then that Marie's temper flared out, kindled by the hour she had been kept waiting. Now it was her turn. It's possible to imagine her as she forced them to listen while she sang one of the really respectable songs of the time, the sort their own wives might sing in their respectable parlours at home. Leering, winking, running her pearls across her teeth, pawing the earth like a rampant stallion, she gave a performance of 'Come into the Garden Maud' that had every conceivable double-meaning – and was quite obscene.

'There,' she concluded, pleased with herself. 'You see? – It's all in the mind.' She tapped her forehead and swept out.

Marie and Music Hall won the day. The earlier triumphs of Mrs Chant and the Puritan Party were never repeated. The Halls were granted the renewal of their licences on 7 October 1896, and the Council even criticized some of the witnesses for their suggestions.

The Era hailed the verdict – 'The Puritan Party – poor feeble creatures – have been defeated all along the line, having relied too much on "broken reeds", whose evidence was fairly riddled by Mr Gill (defending counsel).'

As so often, Marie had the last word : 'I promise that I'll only sing songs like *Home Sweet Home*, if you guarantee the audiences will be as morally unimpeachable as the songs.'

> I always hold with having it
> If you fancy it, that's understood
> And if that's his blooming game
> I intend to do the same
> For a little of what you fancy
> Does you good.

13 Generous to a Fault

Marie was still in her twenties – famous and infamous, popular and reviled, desperately vulnerable. It was one of the tragedies of her life that she seldom had someone to advise her properly; her parents were unable to keep pace with their meteoric daughter, and her brother Johnny who acted for much of the time as her 'Manager' was inadequate. Courtenay had proved hopeless.

Left on her own, Marie reacted to her new notoriety with a wild, compulsive generosity as if she was trying to buy friends, and bursts of defiance as if she wanted to reject them.

It is said that she earned and spent a quarter of a million pounds, but half a million is more likely.

She was paid on Friday nights in gold sovereigns which she swept into her handbag and swept out again to the line of people waiting for her to pass on the way to the stage-door and the street.

A young journalist commented : 'She had scarcely a coin left by the time she got in her carriage.' Chance Newton was critic for *The Referee* and the biographer of Charles Morton. He was the author of the only play that Marie ever appeared in : *The ABC Girl* or *Flossie the Frivolous*. He wrote it for her specially, and at least *The ABC Girl* became a popular song, but the play closed in Wolverhampton where it opened. A pompous comment by Charles Newton on Marie's vulgarity helps to explain the failure : 'I see no need for an artiste to descend to this ceruleanism of song.'

According to Chance Newton, 'The way in which our ever eccentric little friend and star behaved to the chorus girls and men, the supers and other so-called "minor" people: the manner in which she unswervingly helped them, secretly arranging for food and refreshments, for cabs etc, in the small hours of the morning, will never be erased from my memory. Marie never lost, but even made, opportunities to help and succour the needy, the starving and those stricken by death. In fact, Marie was one of the three lady theatrical-cum-variety stars who, not only gave their money lavishly to the poor and suffering, but who gave (as I well know) active service to such unfortunate folk by clearing up their poor rooms, or watching by their bedsides . . .'

All her life she was exploited, shamelessly. In a curious way, her generosity was resented. 'She seems to have been a stupid woman,' a famous Stage Director wrote me recently, 'and her generosity a public show. She was not generous to her own family. She seems to have been as impossible as Marilyn Monroe to the people who served her.'

This is unfair; when she was still a girl she looked after the whole family and moved them into a new house, complete with a pony and trap and a governess for the children.

Remembering her own barefoot days, one of her first salaries was spent on shoes for the children in her street, and this was not a passing gesture. At the beginning of 1894, the *Daily Sketch* referred to her gifts to the children of Shoreditch – 'Many a little heart being gladdened this winter on receipt of a little pink card which says "Please supply . . . with a strong pair of boots and charge to Marie Lloyd gift fund." '

Quibblers point out that someone else had to go to the trouble of fitting the children with shoes which were probably pawned the next day, but others remember Marie descending on Hoxton 'Dressed like a queen – swearing like a Coster, until the children arrived, and then – "here, take this half-a-crown – chilblains? – go to the chemist with this, and then they'll fit".'

In the winter of 1895 she paid for 150 beds in a hostel for the destitute: 'The Gods in the East End Halls know of her kindness of heart' wrote the *Daily Sketch*, describing how she was greeted with cries of 'Wot Cher, Marie!' She was surprisingly popular with other women and once a group of factory girls threw a box of sweets into her brougham, cutting her smartly on the lip. She bought hats for all the women appearing on the same bill, and then took them on to lunch.

'Perhaps they didn't *want* hats!' someone has commented. Equally, they may have been delighted.

Marie was generous to fellow artists in both time and money, realizing the fickleness of fame. Naomi Jacob described how an old and broken-down artist came to the stage-door at Manchester asking if Miss Lloyd would see him. Remembering the days when he had been successful, Marie told him to make himself comfortable and asked the dresser to give him 'a nice drink'. She went off to the dressing-rooms to organize a whip-round. 'Come on, the poor old bloke looks as if he hasn't had a square meal for a week.'

Sharing the bill with Marie was a tight-fisted comedian who grudgingly donated a two-shilling piece. 'Blimey,' exclaimed Marie, staring at the coin, 'how far will two bob go! You're pulling in a hundred and fifty.'

'Might I ask what you're giving him yourself?'

'A quid, and I'll toss you – double or quits! Now then!'

The comedian lost, she added a pound of her own, and returned to the old man chuckling.

Inevitably, she was taken advantage of. When she went on tour she posted back the house-keeping money in cash, and one day after she returned home she went out shopping with her niece. At the first shop the manager took Marie aside and explained with embarrassment that such-and-such a sum was outstanding. The same thing happened in the next shop and every one they went to. Back home, Marie summoned the maid who confessed she'd kept all the money for herself; 'Frances, pack and get out' said Marie.

When her niece asked why she didn't call the police, Marie was horrified – 'Oh no, I don't want to see the poor bitch locked up'. The maid's embezzlement might explain why one shop owner was rash enough to issue a summons against Marie for non-payment. Marie came straight from the Bank and while her driver carried in the money in sacks of half-pennies, she made the manager count every one of them.

Perhaps Marie was one of the few people who are 'generous to a fault'. Certainly she attracted a crowd of spongers, usually women who accepted her generosity as their due, encouraging her to drink, though not to eat. George Godwin, who ghosted her life-story later, wrote to me : 'Among the items I was unable for various reasons to run was one that related how Marie was rewarded for her hospitality. Much of her property vanished when her guests left.' Allied to Marie's generosity, was a rare honesty. One reason that women liked her so much was the lack of airs or pretension. She was beautifully unimpressed.

Naomi Jacob told her a story about Mrs Siddons : how the great actress went to buy a yard of calico and the assistant burst into tears.

'Tears!' said Marie, 'what on earth for?'

'Because Mrs Siddons' voice was so moving, her tones so wonderful.'

'Go on,' said Marie. 'Burst into tears! Give me a yard of Hor-rocks' Longcloth, please. What's there to burst into tears for? I don't care how she said it. I don't believe it.'

With Fred Barnes, a rather effeminate performer whom she called 'Frieda', she was breezily direct. 'What have you done to your lashes?' she asked on one occasion, pointing to his off-stage make-up, 'they look like bloody park railings.'

She was unimpressed, even by Royalty. It's said that when he was Prince of Wales, Edward VII came backstage to see her but was barred from the dressing-room by Bella Burge who didn't recognize him – a pity for they had much in common, especially the love of horse-racing. Marie was delighted at one race-course when she looked up and saw King Edward smiling at her, but apparently he was amused by the extraordinary figure in black beside her, a small old woman from the East End whom Marie had befriended.

Another story, told me by her niece, concerns another Prince of Wales, the future King Edward VIII. She noticed the Prince when she was lunching at Brighton and horrified Mrs Mott by saying she'd go over and introduce herself. He replied graciously that of course he knew who she was, but had never had the honour of seeing her on the stage.

'Then that's an honour you've got to come.'

'Indeed,' he said. 'We're coming to see you tonight.'

But there was one subject on which she was touchy – her age. Not so much the truth of it, as the wild rumours that suggested she was older. Finally she published an advertisement in *The Referee*:

Combined Certificate 1908 – Miss Marie Lloyd. Notice to All – Miss Marie Lloyd has only one daughter and she is not on the stage. In answer to all inquiries – Marie Lloyd, born 12 February 1870. The following are her brothers and sisters and their respective ages :

John Wood (not in the profession), born 17 December 1871.
Alice Lloyd, born 20 October 1873.
Grace Lloyd (not in the profession), born 13 October 1875.
Daisy Wood, born 15 September 1877.
Rosie Lloyd, born 5 June 1879.
Annie Wood (not in the profession), born 25 June 1883.
Sydney Wood, born 1 April 1885.
Maud Wood, born 25 September 1890.

This is final. Will anyone disputing this, kindly apply at Somerset House? Wood is the family name, Lloyd stage ditto.

But she couldn't win. It was said that she issued this to show they were not really her own children.

The pace of Music Hall was killing, literally. Dan Leno went mad, and died at forty-three; Mark Sheridan ('Who were you with Last Night?') shot himself when he thought he was losing his popularity; T. E. Dunville drowned himself; others drowned from drink. Leo Dryden, the singer of the immensely popular *The Miner's Dream of Home* found that patriotism did not pay. He was forced to sing on the streets after pushing handbills through letter boxes, with profits of 11d on his first day. In 1925, he told the Westminster Court – I'm on my beam ends.'

Many of the musicians in the smaller towns had other jobs and played in their spare time. At one town in Lancashire, Dan Leno wanted to try out some classical music for his clog-dance. He was about to hand over the band-parts when the conductor said : 'I don't think we'll need to worry about your music. All th' lads know it very well by now.'

'Yes, but this is something new.'

The conductor studied the sheet-music with surprise : 'By gum! this *is* a bit of something extra.'

'Rather,' said Leno enthusiastically, 'there's some high-toned music among that.'

'There's *lumps* in it! And if I'm not mistaken, there's going to be a bit of trouble over this job.' He consulted his musicians and gave their verdict : 'It's no use Mr Leno. The lads couldn't tackle your job under a matter of three weeks; so unless tha' can be content with th' old la-tum-tiddle, tha' must dance wi'out any music.'

Artists had to be ruthless to survive.

It's hardly surprising that in contrast to her generosity, Marie indulged in outbursts of temper, though they quickly subsided. 'It's better out than in and anyway it relieves my feelings.' At one band-call, Marie lost her temper when the cornet player came in at the wrong moment. She summoned the conductor to her dressing-room and told him : 'Don't let me see his face down there when I go on. D'you think they pay me my salary to have my work mucked about?'

The conductor thought she'd forget, but that evening she sent word that she wouldn't appear if the cornet player was still there. This time the wretched musician himself came to plead his case – 'he was a good musician – he'd been nervous – he was terrified of getting the sack because of his wife and four children ...' Marie relented, told the conductor it was all her fault, and sent presents to the children.

But Marie was not altogether happy in the provinces. It was not true that she was universally popular, as T. S. Eliot implied.

In London they played several Halls a night. In the provinces they had to cope with inexperienced musicians who ran through their numbers briefly on the Monday morning band-call.

Even in the East End Marie could misjudge an audience. One of her severest critics, who managed to remain a friend, was Chance Newton and when Marie told him – 'Chancey, I'm going to the 'Paragon' next Monday. I reckon I shall have to lay it on a bit thick down Whitechapel way, eh what?' he was shocked by her unawareness.

'I warn you,' he replied, 'that if you dare to sing at the Paragon' any of the very shady songs you are now singing in the West End, the East End audiences will balloon you off the stage.'

'My God what rot you talk,' said Marie.

But when she did go on as planned, the audience were so cool that she dashed off-stage smarting with anger. She returned with one of her cleverest character studies and the audience were delighted. They had been hurt to think that Marie should patronize them.

For years, Edward Moss refused to take the risk of engaging her for his Hall in Edinburgh because the capital of Scotland 'disliked vulgarity'. Even in Ardwick, Manchester, she failed to captivate the working-class audience who became decidedly restless during the second house of her last Saturday night. When the show was over and she was dressed to go home, she sauntered on to the empty stage and down to the dulled footlights. Staring into the empty theatre she shouted: 'So this is Ardwick, eh? Well – to hell with the lot of you!'

In Sheffield she clashed verbally with the audience. After a cool reception at the end of the first house, she turned on them angrily. 'You don't like me, well I don't like you. And you know what you can do with your stainless knives and your scissors and your circular saws – you can shove 'm up your arse.' She stormed off to her dressing-room, refusing to go on for the next house. With superb diplomacy, the manager knocked on her door and said he'd come from the audience who wanted to apologize.

'Don't try to schmooze me,' she called.

'They'll do what you say with the knives and the scissors,' he assured her, 'but can they be spared the circular saws?' There was a moment's silence, then a burst of laughter as she relented.

'All right then, play God Save the Queen and tell 'em she's here!'

14 Alec Hurley – the Second Mr Lloyd

In 1896 Marie sailed for South Africa; she was only twenty-six. At the last moment Courtenay reappeared, taking a sudden interest in Marie Junior, and trying to prevent Marie from taking her. While Bella went around telling everyone it was disgraceful that poor little Marie had to be left behind, Johnny Wood smuggled her on board the night before the ship sailed. The next morning Marie and Bella drove up to the quayside and climbed the gangway to the ss *Moor* alone, to the disappointment of the waiting reporters.

The great tours for Music Hall stars were South Africa and Australia. Marie was a triumph and Bella appeared on the bill with Rosie as the 'Sisters Lloyd'. Marie Junior impersonated her mother billed as 'Little Maudie Courtenay'. They caught the attention of the diamond millionaires, Barney Barnato and his nephew Solly Joel. While Barney sent flowers to Bella every night, with a five-pound note tucked inside them, Solly gave the more imaginative gift to Marie of a box of kippers, sent specially from England.

The tour was a triumph in spite of the anti-British feeling that preceded the Boer War. Already her songs were becoming immortal. She gave them *Wink the Other Eye, Twiggy-Vous, Hello, Hello, Hello*. Now she introduced *Oh! Mr Porter* which we are still singing today. Everyone knows the chorus:

> Oh Mr Porter, what shall I do?
> I want to go to Birmingham and they've taken me on to Crewe
> Send me back to London as quickly as you can
> Oh Mr Porter what a silly girl I am

and the lilting tune composed by George Le Brunn. But the verses, written by his brother Thomas Le Brunn, reveal an encounter with 'an old gentleman' who tries to take advantage of her plight, and as far as one can tell succeeds:

The porter would not stop the train, but laughed and said
    you must
Keep your hair on Mary Ann or otherwise you'll bust.
Some old gentleman inside declared that it was hard
Said 'look out of the window Miss and try to call the guard'
Didn't I too, with all my might and nearly balanced over
But my old friend grasped my leg and pulled me back again.
Nearly fainting with the fright I sank into his arms a sight
Went into hysterics, but I cried in vain –
Oh! Mr Porter, what shall I do?
I want to go to Birmingham but they've taken me on to
    Crewe
Send me back to London as quickly as you can
Oh! Mr Porter what a silly girl I am.

and continued her story with growing consternation.

On the voyage back Marie felt that she was rather cold-shouldered by the other First-Class passengers. When they asked her to sing for them on the night of the ship's concert, she replied she had done so already: 'Four times. Twice in the steerage and twice in the Second Class. They loved me, bless 'em.'

'But Miss Lloyd, this is for the First Class.'

'I see,' she is reported to have said coldly, 'but the First-Class passengers failed to recognize me so I'm damned if I'll recognize them.'

Bella Burge was growing up. She was nineteen and though she was no great beauty had already turned down a proposal of marriage from Flo Ziegfeld who had been trying to persuade Marie to appear in one of his shows. Back in England, both she and Marie fell in love. Still appearing with Rosie Lloyd, Bella found herself on the same bill at Gatti's Music Hall as Dick Burge the boxer. Burge had been the champion light-weight in 1891, only to be defeated when he turned middle- and then heavy-weight. He was one of those fighters who are tremendously popular – for guts rather than skill. Now he was thirty-six, unmarked but short of money after losing heavily at the races – which is why he was rat-tat-tatting a punchball in time to a Music Hall song. Bella and Dick fancied each other at once and signed on for another month's engagement.

Meanwhile, Marie had fallen in love with the Coster singer Alec

Hurley who was a friend of Burge and assured Bella – 'You can rely on Dick, he's all right.'

It's assumed that when she left Percy Courtenay Marie promptly married Hurley – this is not the case. Naomi Jacob made a point of stressing that Marie 'never cheated' and 'knew that if, after three years of marriage, things were not particularly happy, they were not likely to improve. She mentally compared her husband with the young Hurley and young Hurley got the better of the comparison ... the divorce went through and Marie Lloyd began life again with Alec Hurley.'

Naomi Jacob skipped *fifteen* crucial years in a sentence! It was not until May 1905 that Marie received the final decree in the divorce from Courtenay and another two years before she married Hurley.

During these years, Marie certainly 'cheated' in so far as she and Hurley lived together as man and wife. She liked him immediately and was determined to get him for herself, even buying a houseboat when she heard that he kept one at Staines, mooring it beside him. Soon the lap of the water, the flow of champagne, banjo music and moonlight had their effect.

Marie and Alec shared a cockney delight in the countryside and eventually she bought two houseboats, The Sunbeam for the day and The Moonbeam which slept seven people. Once The Moonbeam sank in three feet of water and Johnny Wood, woken by Hurley who was still in his pyjamas, describes how Marie, her sisters and Bella waded ashore – 'Then believe me, when it was all over and the clothes were drying on the bushes, we heard all about it from Marie! The beauties of the river, the joys of having houseboats, she had it all ready, I can tell you!' They moved to the village inn where Marie stayed for the rest of the summer. Her doctor told her the river was bad for her health and finally she sold the boats. 'But she always loved it,' said Johnny, 'and I think those days were the happiest of her life.'

By 1900 Marie and Hurley were living together openly and had taken a flat in Southampton Row.

Hurley was a welcome antidote to Courtenay. A year younger than Marie, he was thirty at this date, thick-set and an immensely popular 'man's man'. Above all, he was in Music Hall and a star in his own right though he could never top the bill when he appeared with Marie. He was a Coster singer with Pearly cap, thumbs thrust into waistcoat pockets, and a 'kerchief round his neck. He was in the tradition of Gus Elan (*It's a Great Big Shame!*) but without his scowling genius, and Albert Chevalier (*My Old Dutch*). Hurley was equally sentimental with a song called *Toy* when he placed a midget on his knee who looked up at him saying 'Hello Dad'. According to his niece, Joan Hurley, 'There wasn't a dry seat in the house'. He had a gentle charm all his own, a soft delivery when most performers shouted. Bud Flanagan studied this from the wings, when he was a call-boy, and adapted it for himself later. Hurley's songs included *I 'aint a going to Tell* which was taken up by the Salvation Army as *I 'aint a going to Hell'*, and one number which expressed his own self-effacing personality perfectly :

> I 'aint nobody in perticuler
> Lord bless yer, nobody at all
> I don't want my name in everybody's mouf
> Nor yet posted up on every wall.

Yet, if only from professional pride, it must have rankled that it was always Marie's name 'in everybody's mouf'.

Marie and Alec sailed for Australia in 1901. They did so as 'man and wife', so successfully that it was accepted as a genuine 'honeymoon'. They left behind them a radiant Bella who married Dick in October. Three weeks later her life was shattered when he was arrested for his part in the biggest Bank swindle known up to that time, involving £160,000. Bella now realized why he'd borrowed her own life savings of £300.

But in Australia, it was sunny and triumphant. Marie and Alec opened at Harry Rickards Opera House in Melbourne where Hurley sang an early version of The Lambeth Walk, his answer to the popular craze of the moment – The Cakewalk. The audience was unaware that Marie herself was one of the heavily made-up Coster chorus girls, as he sang the catchy, cockney number :

> You may talk about your Cake Walk
> 'The Lambeth Walk' it knocks 'em all to smithereens.
> It ain't no bloomin' fake walk
> It's the same as we do when we're out a selling greens.
> For we don't want no banjoes, burnt cork or any fake :

> The Lambeth Walk – there ain't no talk
> For that walk takes the cake.

Later there was the usual hum of excitement as they waited for the famous star to appear – and the radiance when she did so.

She sang *Everything in the Garden's Lovely* and *Milly*, a ghastly, stiff little song that only her magic could bring to life:

> Milly from Piccadilly – Milly was adored,
> A rare high stepper, they called her extra pepper
> And they said – Er, er, when'er she walked abroad.
> Milly she isn't silly (ahem)
> Milly (wink) she's all right.

The Australians, less genteel than they are now, but with the same fear of pretension, welcomed Marie's down-to-earth gaiety and gaped at the latest fashions she brought with her. Marie and Alec shared a passion for horse-racing and he bought a string of horses, one of which he named Marie and never won a race. The crowds cheered them wildly whenever they arrived at the course and they were feted throughout the continent. Disliking the restrictions of the hotels, Marie insisted on renting private houses where there was no register or night porter and held parties where everyone was welcome and drink was limitless.

Macqueen Pope suggested that Hurley felt his first disillusion-ment, following in Marie's wake – 'He was a star who had married a planet. Already the seeds of disaster were being sown.' But Pope assumed they were married already, and if Hurley was disillusioned it did not prevent him from marrying her legally five years later.

On their return to England, they did their best to comfort Bella. Alec went to the Old Bailey every day and soon it became obvious that Dick Burge would have to bear the guilt of his two accomplices who had disappeared. 'It's possible he will get two or three years,' Alec warned Bella, who was referred to throughout the trial as 'Bella Lloyd'. Unable to face the trial, she waited tensely for the verdict: 'Ten years, including two years' hard labour', a savage sentence which reduced Burge to tears. Hurley broke the news to Bella and after seeing Dick in the cells, she told Alec and Marie that she was going back to the Halls to save money until his release. She decided to use the name Ella Lane; that of Lloyd had been 'shoved around too much'.

6—MLATMH • •

15 A Cockney Daydream

Courtenay applied for a divorce on 4 November 1904, on the grounds of 'adultery with the Co-respondent Alec Hurley'. Marie was given custody of the child and it hardly bothered her that she was the guilty party – she was not concerned with 'polite society'.

The divorce became absolute on 22 May 1905 and they married on 27 October 1906. It was a warm-hearted wedding. Hurley was described as a bachelor, comedian and thirty-five. Marie as a divorced wife, comedienne and thirty-six. Both gave the same address: 98 King Henry's Road, Hampstead. The witnesses were Sam Poluski, the best man, an eccentric comedian who did a knock-about turn; Alice Lloyd who was married to a Music Hall artist called Tom McNaughton, who did a double-act with his brother; and Marie's brother Johnny.

She arrived at the Registry Office by car about half-past twelve, radiant and smiling, and was greeted by a large crowd of cheering admirers. The local newspaper described it as 'The merriest and most unconventional wedding' that has ever been celebrated by Mr Registrar Bridger of Hampstead, 'there could be no privacy for so popular a favourite as Marie Lloyd'. Marie wore a dress of white cloth trimmed with ermine, an ermine tocque perched on her head, and a bouquet of carnation and lily of the valley in her hand. There were no bridesmaids. 'The most exuberant person present was undoubtedly the bride herself. For everyone there was a smile and a quaint remark, and her spirits compelled her even to indulge in a *pas de deux* now and again.'

They drove to the Gaiety Restaurant afterwards for champagne and speeches. Among the guests were Marie's mother and father; Mr and Mrs Gus Elan; Mrs Fred Karno, and the managers of 'The Tivoli' and 'The Metropolitan'. There were many friends from Music Hall, quick with jokes and puns.

'Why was Alec Hurley?'

'To Marie Lloyd of course.'

'I am the proudest man in the world,' Hurley told the assembly, 'I have got a real gem.' 'He's thinking of my diamonds,' said Marie in a mock stage whisper.

She made a touching little speech. 'I am proud of my husband,' she announced to cheers of approval. 'I hope for a few more years to amuse the public. Then I, and my old man, will settle down at a roadside hostelry, where the motors dash by and nobody stops. Then I will say to my husband – "Come on Alec, put the shutters up and let's be off on 'ossback." ' A delightful cockney daydream. And Marie trotted happily off the stage imitating a horse.

Within a few weeks, Marie was plunged into the excitement of the Music Hall Strike which held its first meeting at their house in Hampstead.

Marie was not directly concerned, she commanded her own terms, but she charged in as champion of the under-dog. For some time, managers had been adding a small 's' after the 'matinée' clause in contracts. Less-important artists, 'the wines and spirits' in tiny print at the bottom of the bill, found themselves playing several matinées for nothing. The agents, ever-sycophantic and anxious not to offend the powerful managers, connived at the trickery. Managers, agents and even the newspapers, treated the threatened strike as a joke but on the evening of 1 January (1907), the London 'Pavilion', 'The Holborn Empire', 'The Oxford' and other Music Halls found they had no orchestra and no artists.

Describing it as 'the most acute crisis that has ever arisen in the amusement world', *The Era* referred to the alliance between the VAF (Variety Artists Federation), the National Union of Stage Employees, and the Amalgamated Musicians' Union, which forbade any artist, stagehand or musician to work in a hall controlled by Walter Gibbons, a magnate whose management 'London Theatres of Variety' controlled a number of halls including the 'Holborn', 'Oxford' and Tivoli' – and later 'The Palladium'. Like most of the other important managers, he received a knighthood.

A first performance was attempted at 'The Holborn' 'by some artists hastily pressed into service. An accompanist was found, and the place of the limelight man was filled by the cinematograph operator with his lantern. The audience took the situation good-temperedly in the main; though there was a noisy demonstration at the opening.' Rusty, long forgotten acts were dragged from obscurity, and old stars tempted out of retirement for a 'comeback'. At 'The Oxford', the manager Mr Blythe-Pratt addressed the audience: 'I am sorry to tell you that the VAF is endeavouring to prevent our artists working here tonight. I regret that it will be quite impossible to present our regular programme, but I am going to put forward an entertainment which I hope will really entertain you.' This consisted of : Mrs Brown Potter who gave a recitation; Mr Ten Thomas who sang a jockey song; Mlle D'Aubigny from the Paris Opera House who sang Tosti's *Goodbye* 'with much taste', a Hungarian violinist and a diminutive Continental mandolinist, 'a decidedly good player'.

Not surprisingly, the liveliest entertainment was found outside the theatre, where pickets distributed leaflets proclaiming :

> MUSIC HALL WAR
> Mr Gibbons says his companies consist
> of picked artistes and musicians.

> MR JOE ELVIN SAYS :
> Unfortunately, he picked them before they were ripe!
> DOWN WITH THE TRUSTS

Artists stopped the passers-by and asked for their support.

'Blacklegs!' Marie shouted gaily at Lockhart's troupe of elephants, the only turn to go on at one Hall, and when Belle Elmore, a second-rate artist, forced her way through pickets to cries of 'Stop her!', Marie shouted back – 'Don't be daft! Let her in and she'll empty the theatre.'

When she heard of another artist who worked twenty halls in one evening, Marie declared. 'When we've won she won't work twenty halls *a year . . .*' and was proved right.

Against such high-spirited opposition, the managers agreed to the modest conditions that were being asked for. It was a personal victory for Marie who had taken an active part from the beginning and contributed generously to the Strike Fund. But like the elephants, the managers never forgot.

There's a postscript to this blackleg appearance of Belle Elmore. At a dinner dance of the Water Rats at the Vaudeville Club in 1910, she was included on the guest list with her husband as 'Doctor and Mrs Crippen' but the doctor arrived with a young girl instead. This was Ethel le Neve and the women present, including Marie, noticed she was wearing some of Belle's jewellery. Knowing Belle, this seemed so suspicious that their gossip over the incident soon alerted the police.

When she was ninety years old, Marie Kendall told me of this dinner and Doctor Crippen :

'He was a little . . . kind of timid man, wore glasses, sleek hair, thin in the face, there was nothing attractive about him but he was always such a nice, kindly little man . . . so . . .' she searched for the right word and pounced on it, 'so . . . *unassuming* !'

At the time of the dinner, the unfortunate Belle had been under the cellar for nineteen days.

By 1910, the cockney daydream of the pub in the country had gone sour, the marriage with Hurley had collapsed after five years. Yet Hurley was to tell Flo' Hastings : 'It was a real love-match. I idolized her.' And, conversely, Alec was the one true love of Marie's life. What went wrong ?

Perhaps they needed the tension of adultery, perhaps marriage was an anti-climax after living together for so long. Hurley could hardly have found the role of 'Mr Lloyd' unendurable for he had worn it comfortably for ten years. A relative blamed Marie's endless round of parties : 'Alec did not care for Romano's and all the swell people Marie knew. He was more of a homebody, he preferred the four-ale bar to the Saloon.'

A simpler and far more devastating reason was the arrival of Bernard Dillon. Born in Tralee in Ireland, he was brought to England as an apprentice jockey when he was thirteen. In 1905 he won the Cambridgeshire and in 1906 the Thousand Guineas and the Grand Prix, his finest race. The next year he brought his family, including four younger brothers and two sisters, to Epsom and soon after that he was invited to one of Marie's famous parties, apparently by Marie Junior. He was raw, short, sexy and shy. Marie barely noticed him at first and only did so on his third visit because he played an accordian, an instrument she viewed with understandable dislike. But when he sang the simple Irish ballads in his rough, untrained voice she stopped to listen. Soon she was obsessed.

'I'm forty, and no woman knows what falling in love can mean until she's forty.' Dillon was twenty-two.

If Dillon had never won the Derby, it might have been different. But he did win it, on Lemberg in 1910. If Marie was The Queen of the Halls, Dillon was now the King of the Turf. When the race was won, with prize money of £6,450, and the shouts had faded, Dillon

MARIE LLOYD

and Music Hall

went back to his Epsom home and fell fast asleep – until Marie arrived with a crowd to drag him back to London while the young brothers and sisters gaped at the grand lady. Marie made no attempt to conceal her infatuation. Once she stood by the rails and called to him as he cantered past. He reined the horse and bent down to kiss her while the crowd cheered.

There comes a point in recklessness when it seems deliberate, as if some inner conscience wants to be discovered – and accused. In particular when the person has a deep sense of morality – like Oscar Wilde and Charles Dickens. When André Gide met Wilde, after he'd been released from prison, he reminded him of their last meeting in Algiers when Wilde 'almost predicted the catastrophe'. 'Oh! Of course,' said Wilde, 'of course, I knew that there would be a catastrophe – that one or another, I was expecting it. It had to end that way. Just imagine: it wasn't possible to go any further; and it couldn't last.'

Dickens, too, charged headlong into the very scandal he was fearing when he published his extraordinary statements against his wife in his own newspaper, as if his guilt was too terrible not to be shared.

In the same way, Marie was swept along the road to disaster, infatuated with a younger person. At a time when many people were shocked even by divorce, she lived openly with Dillon using no discretion.

Leslie Bell suggests that pride prevented a reconciliation with Hurley, that Bella beseeched her: 'Don't you know what you're doing to yourselves? That's not what you want and well you know it.' While Dick told Alec: 'Go and see her and straighten things out', to which he replied bitterly: 'No. If that's what Marie wants, then let her get on with it.'

Naomi Jacob said that Hurley was too weak. This is denied by his niece Joan Hurley: 'He was anything but weak. He'd get up at six in the morning and run across Hampstead Heath. He dived off the Pier in Brighton. That's not a weak person. Weak in love, maybe, but who isn't?' Perhaps that is what Naomi Jacob meant.

Any chance of a reconciliation was hindered by Hurley's constant tours in the provinces and overseas, where at least he had the consolation of being top of the bill. Once Flo Hastings heard Marie warn him: 'You'll do it one day too much, Alec. You'll come home and there'll be no home there.' It was not an idle threat. Joan Hurley remembers being taken to Waterloo Station by her family to welcome

Uncle Alec from a tour of South Africa and Australia. He showed them a big pendant stone, the size of an egg, with a diamond in the centre, which he brought for Marie. He asked for her eagerly and the family broke the news – 'She's left you.' Hurley gave the pendant to Joan's younger sister, little Rosie Hurley, who climbed on a bench in the refreshment room and sang: 'You can get a sweetheart any day, but not another mother!'

This was one of the rare occasions when Marie behaved callously. Hurley drove to their former home near Regent's Park only to find it stripped, his trunk packed and waiting in the empty hall.

Dillon was disastrous for Marie, but so was she for him. In 1911 the Jockey Club took away his licence, and his career. His brother, who still lives in Epsom, says that Bernard owned some horses and bet on them. He had the bad luck to owe some money to a trainer who exposed him: 'Many jockeys did the same, but he was found out. They robbed him and he turned after that.' The whole justification of Dillon's life, his passion and his skill had been taken away. The discipline of racing was removed and so was the struggle to keep down his weight – now he could drink as freely as he wished.

This same year – 1911, a divorce case was started between Marie and Hurley, but though it came before judge Sir Samuel Evans, neither party appeared and it was dropped at the last moment. Perhaps Hurley, who was a Catholic, hoped the infatuation would pass.

Hurley had moved into 'Jack Straw's Castle' in Hampstead, where the owner was a friend, and he started to drink heavily. Daisy Stratton, a Music Hall star of the First World War, and eighty-five when I met her, remembered going there one lunchtime with Marie. Hurley was sitting by himself at the other end of the long bar.

'Hullo Alec' called Marie.

Hurley ignored her; just sat there looking in front of him.

'Have a drink?' she asked.

Then he turned round and looked at her. 'With *you*?' he said with contempt, and walked out.

16 The Scandal of the Royal Command

Nowadays, the Royal Command Performance is an accepted if boring annual event. In 1912 it was a sensation. This was the first real Royal Command and it was held especially for Music Hall.

For some time, Sir Edward Moss had been trying to arrange a special performance for Their Majesties at the 'Empire' in Edinburgh, which he was especially proud of and regarded as the 'spiritual home' of the Moss Empire Circuit. A date was fixed for the summer of 1911, but his ambitions were wrecked on the night of 9 May, when the 'Empire' starred an American called Sigmund Neuberger, who had been born in Munich, and travelled with an animal show as The Great Lafayette. He was famous as an illusionist. The week started badly with the death on Monday of his favourite dog 'Beauty', a gift from his friend Houdini, and the refusal of the local authorities to bury Beauty in the Piershill Cemetery. On the Thursday night, Lafayette was holding a flaming torch which set fire to the curtain, which was not fire-proofed. The blaze spread rapidly and Lafayette jumped on the burning stage to stop the panic, while a trombonist played God Save the King. Lafayette was burnt to death with nine others. There were rumours that he was seen outside, returning to the blaze to rescue or shoot one of the wild animals. The confusion was partly due to a 'double' in his act, who was actually buried as Lafayette until the other charred body was found with rings on the fingers which proved the real Lafayette's identity. He was buried in a private vault at Piershill with the remains of Beauty.

The loss of the 'Empire' was a deep shock to Moss. It ended his ambitions for a Royal Command in Edinburgh and even hastened the end of his life, for he died a few months after the Royal Command in London the following year, now transferred to London.

Moss was one of the great powers of the halls, and like Stoll, De Frece, Barrasford and Thornton, he started in the North – in Greenock. At his peak he controlled thirty-three halls. In 1898, to avoid a clash of interests, he joined forces with Oswald Stoll and they built the new Empire Palace in Nottingham together with Stoll as Managing Director. They issued this statement :

> Messrs Moss and Stoll control Theatres in Edinburgh, Glasgow, Newcastle, Sheffield, Liverpool, Hull, Birmingham, Cardiff, Swansea and Newport, thus being in a position to offer a separate engagement for each of so many halls in the Tour, the Management have unusual facilities for procuring those artists whose services Managers, unable to make very tempting offers, *are compelled to do without.*

This flagrant monopoly led to an exclusive 'barring clause' by the big combines. As the Tour was essential to Music Hall artists, their offer was irresistible to some – under any terms – and ruinous to others. Several independent halls couldn't face such competition and closed. This was one reason for the Variety Artists Strike in 1907.

In 1910, anxious to be his own master, Stoll resigned as Managing Director of the Moss Syndicate – another blow to Moss – and in 1912 he took over the supervision of the Royal Command with all the enthusiasm that Moss had lost. The glee of Stoll and the other managers was awful as their day of honour approached. 'At last,' Oswald Stoll proclaimed unctuously, 'the Cinderella of the Arts has come to the Ball.'

Stoll was a strange impressario – unsympathetic yet dedicated. His love of Music Hall cannot be doubted, yet he didn't seem to understand it. Like the woman who marries a reprobate, he wanted to change and reform the very qualities that attracted him in the first place.

He was born in Melbourne, Australia, but was brought up in Liverpool where his widowed mother married a Danish waxworks proprietor called John Stoll – and adopted his name. The waxworks and a 'beer and sawdust' music hall were run in the Parthenon Rooms and when his step-father died suddenly in 1880, Oswald took over at the age of fourteen and ran the place with his mother. He made the Parthenon famous. He looked so young that sometimes he pretended he was the office boy and disappeared into the office, which was empty, for the necessary signatures and approval of his 'boss'. Later he fell in love with one of the most popular of his artists, Vesta Tilley, but she married his Liverpool rival Walter de Frece.

It's claimed he was so distressed that he moved south to forget the association and started the 'Cardiff Empire', but when he ran into trouble it was Vesta Tilley who helped him out by appearing twice-nightly, an innovation then, for a week at a nominal salary. Success followed and the Stoll 'Tour' had begun.

He built the colossal 'Coliseum' in London in 1904 and cherished it through early years of artistic and financial disaster. He began with lavish spectacles on the immense revolving stages, such as Derby Day, but one of the horses slipped and threw the jockey who was killed. After several more accidents, the 'Coliseum' was nick-named 'The Morgueseum'. When the company went into early bankruptcy in 1906, Stoll bought the 'Coliseum' back after an unsuccessful auction, which earned him a lingering reputation for 'sharp practice'. A minor mishap involved Stoll's subservience to the idea of Royalty. Quite unnecessarily, there was a separate entrance for The Royal Family and a special royal train was built to carry them the few yards from the lift to the Royal Box. Edward VII tried it for the first time but it refused to work. He added to the general humiliation by emerging merrily, singing a Marie Lloyd refain – 'Eh, What, What, What!'

Technically, the 'Coliseum' was a Music Hall but Stoll saw it as something grander. There were no drinking bars and there were signs in the dressing-rooms : *Please do not* use *any strong language here* and *Coarseness and Vulgarity are not allowed in the Coliseum.* Also – *Gentlemen of the chorus are not allowed to take their whips to the dressing-rooms.* There were four shows a day.

Unattractive, with gold pince-nez, deploring the use of 'expletives', Stoll was not only a teetotaller but a non-smoker. He patrolled 'The Coliseum' picking up cigar ends off the carpet with the rebuke to the customer – 'Pardon me sir, but you wouldn't have done that in your own home would you?'

When an artist complained about his position as last on the bill, explaining that he lived outside London and it was hard to find transport so late, Stoll had the simple solution : 'Move.' When a Manager dared to criticize him, Stoll warned 'Do not ever dare tell me that I am wrong. If it happens again you will be dismissed.' A considerable time later, the man had forgotten the incident and pointed out another mistake. 'Mr Manager,' said Stoll, 'I told you once before never to dispute my orders. Kindly now go and draw three months' salary from the cashier in lieu of notice.'

And when he lowered the curtain on Sophie Tucker, she yelled :

'Mr Stoll you shouldn't be the Manager of a Vaudeville Theatre. You should be a Bishop!'

Yet Stoll was an innovator. In his own unendearing way, he loved Music Hall as much as Marie. Unfortunately he was ashamed of its honest vulgarity and tried to improve it into something 'posh' – everything it was not.

In between such traditional turns as George Robey, whose double-meanings seemed to escape him, he slipped in such startling material as a farce by Cocteau (1912) with masks by Dufy, and Russian ballet with Karsavina, in 1909. Nijinsky and Pavlova were billed for 'The Coliseum', but played the 'Palace'; in 1918, Lopokova followed 'The Educated Apes in Fokines' – Cleopatra.

Stoll can take the credit of putting up thousands of pounds for Diaghilev's splendid but unfashionable production of The Sleeping Princess, which failed after 105 performances at the 'Alhambra' in 1921. But to his everlasting discredit he impounded the sets by Bakst and refused to allow them to be sent to Paris. After three years of wandering, Diaghilev agreed to play twenty-four weeks at the 'Coliseum' if he could have the properties back, but when they were unearthed from storage they were rotten with damp and half-eaten by rats.

In many ways, Stoll thought of 'The Coliseum' as a theatre rather than a hall. Edith Evans made her début there in The Merry Wives of Windsor, John Gielgud played a season of Romeo and Juliet which did badly, and master Noël Coward appeared in A Little Fowl Play at the age of twelve. This was after Stoll had in fact acquired a theatre licence; his was the last battle under the 1843 Act between theatres and halls, and yet again Shakespeare was the offender. Rival theatrical managers insisted that Shakespearian extracts be limited to half-an-hour. When he defied this he had to appear in court with Sir Seymour Hicks who had been playing Richard III. At last in 1912, the year of the Royal Command, he won a theatre licence from the Lord Chamberlain which allowed him to stage plays as well as Music Hall. 'Nothing but good is likely to come from the gradual obliteration of the old boundary between Music Hall and the theatre' wrote William Archer at the time. Yet in removing the boundary, the individuality of Music Hall was blurred.

Stoll asked Sarah Bernhardt to play 'The Coliseum' in 1910; (as a single performer on her own she was unaffected by the Act of 1843.) But she was so repelled by the thought of performing animals that she cabled back : 'Not after the monkeys'. He persuaded her with a record salary of £1,000 a week and an eighty-foot red Turkey carpet laid from her dressing-room to the stage so she wouldn't have to tread the same boards as the elephants that preceded her. At the age of seventy, she impersonated a youth of nineteen in the second act of L'Aiglon. She returned in 1911, 1912, 1913 and even 1916, after her leg had been amputated, with a passionate performance in French of a dying soldier. What stamina the 'Coliseum' audience had, to survive this – or the shortened version of Hamlet, also in French.

It was at a dinner at 'The Lyceum', given for Bernhardt by Irving, that someone asked her whom she thought was the greatest actress on the English stage. This was hardly tactful, in view of Ellen Terry's association with the 'Lyceum', and when Bernhardt replied 'Marie Lloyd' there was a shocked silence. Afterwards it was suggested that this might have been a joke, or a deliberate criticism of Ellen Terry. James Agate tried to prove, rather confusingly, that she was referring to a minor actress who also had the name of 'Marie Lloyd'. This is hardly convincing in view of Bernhardt's comments in a later interview when she listed the things she liked most in London : The Tower, The Crystal Palace, The Houses of Parliament and the Albert Memorial – 'but you happen to have only one woman of genius on your stage and that is Marie Lloyd.'

The two women were introduced by the theatrical costumier Willie Clarkson while Marie was doing an impersonation of Bernhardt at 'The Tivoli'. The two women exchanged photographs : Marie was shown in her Bernhardt make-up, and the French actress inscribed hers to – 'The Bernhardt of the Halls'.

Stoll never invited Marie to play at 'The Coliseum'. He thought her too great a risk for his beloved theatre where 'you could safely take your maiden aunt to'. But in spite of her marriage to de Frece, Vesta Tilley was always welcome and Stoll even wrote songs for her.

Now Stoll, de Frece and Moss were in charge of the arrangements for the Royal Command and the Music Hall waited eagerly. The list was published of the artists chosen to appear before the King and Queen and there was uproar. Marie Lloyd's name wasn't on it. The most popular star of Music Hall was out. To add further insult, she was not invited to the finale, a vast 'Variety Garden Party' when 142 artists were to walk on to represent the profession – she was considered too risky even for that.

The general public was bewildered. Newspapers buzzed with the scandal, printing letters of protest: 'I for one, will never accept the performance – grand though it necessarily must be, as really representative. Marie Lloyd must ever be our representative comedienne on the halls . . . One cannot, of course, please everybody. The Committee could not be expected to work miracles, but, as one behind the lights, I can see that a great wave of favouritism has burst in on the whole concern, and one can see which members of the Committee had the most of 'the Day' when the list is perused. I hear some talk of a revision: I hope it will come about and that the Committee own up to their blunder, or their undue slights . . .' But there was no revision.

Marie was deeply hurt. She assumed her name had been removed from the list and told Bella Burge: 'I won't let them get away with it. You'll see what'll happen if they don't put me back on the list.' It never occurred to her that she might not have been on it in the first place. An Executive Committee had chosen the artists and submitted the list to the Committee who passed it on to Buckingham Palace. Someone, somewhere along the line had said 'No' to Marie Lloyd, or it had been accepted from the start that such a woman would be unacceptable. The managers were in a tizzy of sycophancy and were not going to jeopardize the evening – or their knighthoods – in any way. At the same time they had the satisfaction of revenge for the Strike and her years of defiance.

For Marie it was bitter public humiliation.

There were two other, inexplicable omissions: Eugene Stratton and Albert Chevalier. The case of Chevalier was odd for he had appeared privately before the Royal Family once before. Now he took a whole page in *The Era* to advertise his grievance, quoting *The Morning Post*: 'Historically as well as artistically his omission is a blunder of the first magnitude.'

Like the Covent Garden porter in the song, who came into 'a bit o'splosh, and he dunno where 'e are', Music Hall was getting above itself. On the morning of the Command, Stoll inserted an advertisement in *The Era* which was a warning to the profession: 'Coarseness, vulgarity etc are not allowed. The licensing authorities forbid this, and the great majority of the public resent it. This intimation is rendered necessary only by a few artists.'

The young manager of 'The Palace', Alfred Butt, referred to the 're-generation of the Music Hall', and an editorial in *The Era* hailed the day as representing: 'the progress of the Music Hall from something which respectable people used to go to furtively to a place where majesty itself now goes openly.

'The old Music Hall was really a survival of grubby Bohemianism, a lineal descendant of the "Cider Cellar" and the tavern sing-song.

'It had its good points and some courageous souls, even now, regret it, or make the pretence that they do. For I think it is but a pretence, and that only those who have a morbidly conventional horror of being thought conventional really lament the Music Hall of the chairman, his mallet, beer, orange peel, grubbiness, and the reek of shag. They pretend to think that the virtue has gone out of Music Halls ever since people in evening dress began to fill the stalls, and ever since thick pile carpets began to replace a sawdusty and salivaceous covering.

'But now,' exulted Harold Owen, the writer of the editorial, 'the progress of the Music Halls from dinginess and disrepute to brightness and respectability, is one of the most reassuring traits of the times.

'Gone is the pathetic serio-comic, with her unlovely lyrics and amorous inanities; gone, the red-nosed comedian; gone the type of humour that centred round the lodger.

'The Music Hall, in fact has achieved the triumph of becoming respectable and ceasing to be dull.'

Yet what could be duller than respectable Music Hall? It was never intended for the King and Queen, nor for Cocteau and Pavlova.

If Marie had appeared that evening at the Royal Command it would have been wrong: it wasn't the tradition of Music Hall that was being honoured, but a new form of Variety.

The Command began on a Monday evening at 8.5 before a welter of Royalty: the Grand Duchess George of Russia, Princess Henry of Battenberg, and Princess Christian were received by Butt at the Royal entrance. Even Conan Doyle who reported the evening, succumbed to obeisance describing King George v as a 'lover of true Bohemianism'. He described the inside of the theatre, glowing with red roses, as a 'floral fairyland' but unfortunately the show itself was chilly. Just as they are today the artists were stiff and indulged in that embarrassing play to the Royal Box which the Royal Family must find more tedious than anyone.

Harry Tate said afterwards: 'I was all right after I had got out the line about taking my son back to the Naval College, with the accent on the "Naval". The King smiled and then I was quite comfortable.'

Happy Fanny Fields though 'fresh and bonny as ever', was so nervous that she made the mistake of telling the audience : 'I'm suffering just as much as you are.'

Wilkie Bard was described as 'dreadfully dull' by the *Daily Mail*, and Pippax and Paulo were trembling with anxiety.

Chirgwin – 'The One-Eyed Kaffir' – a performer in the true Music Hall tradition, was out of his element. 'Somehow or other,' reported *The Daily Chronicle*, 'before that brilliant company, Mr Chirgwin's performance on the one-stringed gramophone-fiddle was a curious reminder of the music-hall's unambitious days'. He cracked a joke towards the Royal Box – 'but somehow or other it had not quite the answering laugh from the highest quarter that was expected.

' "Sorry it didn't go" said Mr Chirgwin, like the fine old fellow that he is.' Dreadfully similar to today.

Ida Crispi walked out at rehearsals when Stoll said it wouldn't be 'nice' to have her rolled up in a carpet at the end of Yankee Tangle, and Little Tich was so nervous that he refused to go on at the end when Harry Claff in a suit of white shining armour, and a white helmet (strangely like a policeman's) led the whole company in the national anthem.

But the greatest disappointment was one that must have been sweet to Marie.

Throughout the evening, with every act, every eye was turned to the Royal Box particularly to Queen Mary, wrote *The Chronicle*, 'for it was she who was to answer the really vital question as to whether the mothers of England are to sanction the Music Hall not only for their husbands', sons', and daughters' entertainment, but for their own.'

The moment of disapproval arrived, when Queen Mary leant forward and advised the other regal ladies in the box to avert their eyes from the sight of Vesta Tilley in trousers.

This rebuke has been denied. Georgie Wood who was there told me : 'That's an idiotic story, the Queen was far too gracious a lady to have been so rude.'

But the newspapers imply that it *did* happen. *The Chronicle* reported : 'So far as Queen Mary and the other Royal ladies were concerned, one little fact was curiously inescapable. They obviously did not like the appearance of Miss Vesta Tilley in her familiar male costume as the inimitable Algy. Queen Mary, and the Grand Duchess George of Russia, consulted their programmes almost severely throughout the song, and studiedly looked away from the stage ... an expression on Queen Mary's face that she does not approve of actresses appearing in masculine clothes.'

The Queen was not amused. To make it still more embarrassing, apart from the fact that Vesta Tilley was married to Walter de Frece who was partly responsible for the evening, she sang a song that had been written for her especially by Oswald Stoll – *Mary and John* which made no impression whatever.

Where was Marie?

Only a couple of hundred yards away, at the other end of Shaftesbury Avenue, staging her own show at the 'London Pavilion' before a three-weeks' season in Paris.

It would be nice to think that she gave the performance of her life, urged on by the loyal crowd of supporters who had returned their ten-guinea tickets for the Command. Surprisingly, in view of her declarations of loyalty, Naomi Jacob was at the 'Palace' but Bella and Dick were at the 'Pavilion' and Hurley slipped in unnoticed and stood at the back. Marie was billed with new songs – *One thing leads to another* and *Coster girl in Paris,* and (perhaps) she gave them such additional favourites as *Oh Mr Porter,* and *The Boy I Love is up in the Gallery.* Certainly her performance was more lively than the ritual at the 'Palace'. Far from being subdued, Marie fought back with the old defiance. She was billed as *'Queen of Comedy'.*

Outside, the theatre had special strips pasted across the posters with the proud proclamation

EVERY PERFORMANCE BY MARIE LLOYD
IS A COMMAND PERFORMANCE

BY ORDER OF THE BRITISH PUBLIC

Alfred Butt, the Manager of 'The Palace', and Walter de Frece, received their knighthoods in 1919. The accolade seemed to go to Sir Walter's head. He resigned as Managing Director of the Varieties Controlling Company and stood for Parliament; he was elected MP for Ashton-under-Lyne in 1924. It is said that he avoided his old associates in Music Hall and was given the nickname – Sir Altered de Frece. Because of his entry into politics, Vesta Tilley, now a

Lady, retired from the stage after a grand farewell performance at 'The Coliseum' with seventeen curtain calls and a ladder of fame, made of violets, behind her. Later she made her home in the South of France and died there in 1952 at the age of eighty-eight. It's astonishing to think that she made her first performance, admittedly at the age of four, as far back as 1868.

She published a book of memoirs, but there is only one brief reference to Marie as 'That very great artist'.

17 Arrest in New York

With Dillon disqualified from racing and Marie smarting from the humiliation of the Royal Command, they must have felt a tremendous relief when they sailed for America in 1913, apart from the promise of fifteen hundred dollars a week for a six-month tour.

Her sister Alice had left on the *Mauretania* the week before, on the way to the Pacific Coast and Australia. A New York paper, lamenting Alice's short stay, was consoled by the news that 'Marie Lloyd will soon be with us again. Vaudeville is none the less enjoyable for a dash of ginger!'

Marie was still married to Alec Hurley and not divorced as usually stated. Fruitless efforts to trace such a divorce, finally made me realize that there never was one.

In *Queen of the Music Halls,* Macqueen Pope states: 'In 1910, Alec Hurley sued for divorce. He named Bernard Dillon as co-respondent, and he won the case.' But in fairness to Pope he did say; 'I have made no attempt to write an authoritative, chronological and exhaustively detailed story of the life of Marie Lloyd. It is very doubtful if such a book could be written in a satisfactory manner. The people of Music Hall did not leave the pile of documentation that their brethren of the Theatre accumulate.'

This is all too true, but as Marie herself pointed out in her advertisement in *The Referee*, there was always Somerset House for the skeleton fact.

Marie and Bernard sailed as 'Mr and Mrs Dillon'. It may well have been her success in travelling as 'Mrs Hurley' years before, when she was still Mrs Courtenay, that made her repeat the deception. What made it slightly nasty this time was that Hurley was dying at 'Jack Straw's' in Hampstead. He was thinking in terms of a comeback – 'Don't you think you've gone back ten years in life if you hear me singing *My Boy Jimmy* some night', he told a journalist. But though he was still popular he was drinking heavily and managers were reluctant to book him.

Alice was waiting at the Pier to greet the *Olympic* which docked with all the drama of a liner's arrival. For Marie there was an onslaught of photographers and press, including an English journalist who arrived late and breathless and explained that he hadn't been able to find Marie's cabin because her name wasn't on the passenger list.

'It's under the Ds,' she said, and the man wandered off puzzled.

Having passed an immigration check on board, they were literally under a large D on the quayside beside a mass of luggage, about to be cleared by the Customs and off to the Astor Hotel, when an immigration inspector hurried up with the journalist and called Marie aside. Solemnly, he told her that the best way out of an unpleasant situation was to tell the truth about her relationship with Dillon.

'Is this man,' he stabbed a finger at Dillon, 'your lawful husband?'

Marie had to admit they were not legally married. The inspector informed her he had no alternative but must stop them from going ashore. As Ellis Island was overcrowded, he gave them permission to stay on the *Olympic* but they would have to report to the Board in the morning who would decide if she was allowed to enter America.

At this new public humiliation, Marie broke down and wept. Sister Alice tried to comfort her and Marie opened a valise and brought out a bottle of champagne. After she fortified herself with a glass or two, she climbed back on board followed up the gangway by Dillon.

Armed with five lawyers, they were taken from the *Olympic* to Ellis Island in the morning and their case was heard first, before 700 others. The enquiry was held behind closed doors and even the lawyers were refused admittance. Marie explained to the officials that they intended to be married as soon as possible. She added that if it hadn't been for the intervention of the King's Proctor, they would now be Mr and Mrs Dillon in reality as well as name.

Possibly feeling that if she wasn't good enough for the King's Proctor she wasn't good enough for them, the officials told her that she would be deported with Dillon for 'moral turpitude' and interned on Ellis Island until the *Olympic* sailed the following Saturday. Dillon was charged under the White Slave Act of America 'with taking to the country a woman who is not his wife'. Miss Lloyd was accused of being 'a passive agent'.

As she was taken off under close arrest, Marie was reported as 'hysterical'.

MARIE LLOYD
and Music Hall

'I shall never forget my feelings when the key was turned on me at Ellis Island,' she wrote afterwards. 'I suffered the tortures of hell. They placed me in solitary confinement, and I stayed there looking through iron bars at the Statue of Liberty. What irony! The statue ought to be pulled down. It is a standing lie.

'As for Ellis Island, it is horrible, horrible, horrible! Why! I wouldn't put pigs there. There is not an atom of comfort and the stench is overwhelming. Dillon was herded with thirty scarcely human immigrants of various nationalities. For myself, for a short time, I went raving mad and had to be attended by the doctor. I really thought I should die.'

To a journalist, who asked her later what she thought of America, she pointed to the Statue of Liberty and exclaimed: 'I love your sense of humour!'

Indeed, the words engraved on the base of the Statue must have been bitter to the 15,000 people who were ordered back to Europe every year after being refused permission to land:

> Give me your tired, your poor, Your huddled masses yearn-
> ing to be free,
> The wretched refuse of your teeming shore, Send these
> the homeless,
> Tempest-tossed to me.

While Dillon was taken to a dormitory filled with 'unwashed Lithuanians', Marie was given a small room of her own with a cot and chair, where she could have meals from the kitchens supplying the Island's staff. She could smoke and go to the immigrants' counter for pie, cider, or some sandwiches for a shilling (not sold singly). She was allowed to exercise on the roof of the building and her maid could visit her in the day, though not stay overnight. Though she was virtually in prison, she got the special treatment that Maxim Gorky and the ex-President of Venezuela had enjoyed while their appeals were being heard and as they had been allowed to land, this was encouraging. Her lawyers in New York were fighting hard for an appeal claiming she had already been passed by the immigration officer on the *Olympic* and that the Board could not revoke a decision of one of its own men. They also pointed out the precedent of a lady acrobat who had been detained with her 'friend', but was released to fulfil her engagement.

Cables of sympathy poured in from England, but the *New York Globe* replied coldly to the criticism : 'America lays no claim to being more moral than other civilized nations. It numbers among its vast population moral and immoral, but the moral far outnumber the immoral, and a sense of public decency, which we trust is not lacking in England, forbids the flaunting of one's immorality in public. That is all there is to this very disagreeable affair.'

It was a hurtful moment for Hurley, especially when he was shown the interview Marie gave on Ellis Island proclaiming her love for Dillon : 'There was no legal way I could marry Dillon after we found we loved each other,' she said. 'All our friends and people generally in England have understood our position, and regarded us as husband and wife. We have lived together and for each other, and are as loyal and faithful to each other as man and wife can be. We have in fact regarded ourselves as married.'

With dignity, Hurley declined to comment to reporters but described the action of the officials as foolish and added – 'I am very sorry it has happened.'

On the Friday night, Marie and Dillon left Ellis Island and boarded the *Olympic*, booking their return to England. Her temper flared as she snapped at reporters – 'You call this a free country and yet there is not another country on earth that would expose a defenceless woman to such public ignominy, ridicule and mortification. The same heartless ruling, if applied to grand opera singers and theatrical stars, would bar some of the greatest artists from your country.' She gave her parting shot – 'I have decided never again to appear before the American public.'

The next morning as the *Olympic* was about to sail, Marie and Dillon, Tom and Alice MacNaughton, made their emotional farewells. A car raced up the quayside and Pat Casey, Marie's Booking Agent for the tour ran to the group to tell them of a last-minute reprieve. The Washington Board of Inquiry had decided not to uphold the Ellis Island order at the last moment – but Marie had to endure the mortification of further conditions : she was only allowed to stay if she gave bail for £300 each for Dillon and herself, promised to be of good behaviour, and leave the following March. There was the extra stipulation that she and Dillon would have to stay in 'separate establishments'. For a moment Marie wavered. She told one of the reporters that if she had her own way she'd only stay a week in America, just to show she wasn't ashamed. Pat Casey pleaded and by eleven o'clock the vows of the previous evening were forgotten.

'I have decided to stay here,' she announced, but couldn't help adding: 'I think it's a shame anyway. I thought this was a free country.'

Then with whoops of joy, the group jumped into Casey's car and headed for Broadway and a celebration lunch.

Later, her attorney Moses Grossman, issued the following statement: 'Marie Lloyd is delighted with the reversal of the order of the Court . . . she has resented the manner of her treatment by the American officials, but was overjoyed when she read that the people of London, who idolize her, had called mass meetings to protest against the conduct of these officials. She hopes that before 1 March she may obtain a complete reversal of the decision of the Board of Inquiry.'

That evening, Marie stayed with her sister Alice at her home in 267 West 89th Street. Followed by reporters she refused to say anything, particularly the whereabouts of Dillon. He was keeping the 'conventional distance' that the conditions demanded. To reporters he was surprisingly discreet and told them he had given up racing because he was too stout.

When Marie opened in New York, the stewards from the *Olympic* – back from their next voyage – crowded the gallery and gave her a cheering reception.

Alec Hurley died in London two months later, on 6 December 1913. He had returned from Glasgow a week earlier and the doctors found he was suffering from double-pneumonia. He was forty-two.

Inevitably, the obituaries were headed – *Miss Marie Lloyd's husband dead* – but one described him as the 'Kindly Comedian a man who made many friends and of whom none spoke evil.'

The *Daily Mirror* stressed his love of domesticity: 'He had the domestic temperament, and all the domestic ideals. Home, a fireside, children, pets, and small acts of kindness were subjects that would always warm his conversation to a glow of enthusiasm.' In other words, *not* a night out at 'Romano's'.

It is claimed that his last words were of Marie. 'Tell Marie,' recorded Macqueen Pope, 'that I love her as much now as the first day I saw her. She knows how much that is.'

According to Leslie Bell, he told Bella Burge: 'I'll not see Marie again, Bella, but you'll tell her for me, won't you? There's only been her all the time. Say that and give her my love.'

The news was broken to Marie when she was playing in Chicago. Marie sent a wreath to be placed inside the coffin away from gossipping eyes, with the card 'Until we meet again'. Deeply upset by the loss of their friend, Dick and Bella Burge found out what debts he'd left behind and settled them. 'Alec was never a welsher,' said Dick, 'I wouldn't want that said about him.'

Meanwhile, Marie and Dillon trailed unhappily across America and Canada. In Alberta she is supposed to have horsewhipped an editor who wrote that she talked like a scrubwoman and looked like a grandmother. She left his office with the angry promise that she would be remembered long after he was forgotten.

But crowds followed her everywhere. She was invited to the christening of a child named after her, and was called to the window to make a speech to the people below. Flattered, she told the guests afterwards: 'They know the Queen when they see one. Queen of Variety, don't you know'. Her conceit was so totally lacking in modesty on such occasions, that it was almost disarming.

The manager of one theatre she was appearing in actually signed a petition against her and tried to prevent her from going on, but she swept past him to cheers from the audience.

Now she was free to marry Dillon and end their daily humiliation. They crossed the border again and married at the British Consulate at Portland, Oregon on 21 February 1914. Dillon gave his residence as the Portland Hotel and his age as twenty-nine. Marie gave the Multnomah Hotel and her age as thirty-seven. For her first marriage she added one year; for her third she had subtracted seven.

Yet even with this legality they did not find freedom. A report in a British newspaper on 29 May said 'She will be with us again early in June, as the official meddlers in America declare that she must leave America before the first of the month. (Which was longer than Washington had stated.) But if the authorities have made consumate fools of themselves, the American public have been very kind.'

Marie sailed for England where 'the boys, young and old, will be glad to see her again' and Waterloo Station was crowded with friends lining the platform to see her alight on Dillon's arm. Then she hurried by car to her house in Golders Green where the white balconies fluttered with Union Jacks. She paused in the doorway to wave at the crowd. She was home at last.

Charles Reed, the manager of the local Golders Green Hippodrome, had booked her for her first reappearance. In spite of a cold

MARIE LLOYD
and Music Hall

'the applause was so loud and long that one realized the truth of the description in the programme that she is London's favourite comedienne.' She sang three favourites including *The Coster Honeymoon in Paris*, in which she purposely dropped her glove and tried to pick it up again in a very tight skirt, and ended with a song that was really Ella Retford's *Who paid the rent for Mrs Rip Van Winkle?* which had been a success in America, and made a little speech. The Americans, she said, were not such a bad lot, but she was very glad to be back in dear old England.

Within a fortnight, Archduke Ferdinand was assassinated at Sarajevo, and soon England was at war.

Music Hall indulged in a splurge of patriotism. Vesta Tilley marched on the stage of 'The Coliseum', a splendid set of Waterloo Station 'straight from the front', returning for 'six days home on leave' with the mud of Flanders on her boots, a German helmet in her hand, and the startling cry: 'Gurls! If you'd like to love a soldier, you can all love me.'

Her uniforms and military songs, such as her old favourite *Jolly good luck to the girl who loves a soldier* took on a new meaning.

Marie's contribution was equally typical:

> I do like you Cockey when you've got your khaki on
> I do feel so proud of you, I do honour bright
> I'm going to give you an extra cuddle tonight.

Marie visited hospitals and halls and appeared 'Sunday after Sunday', as Sir Seymour Hicks recalled, at his concerts for soldiers at the 'Princes Theatre'. Naomi Jacob wrote emotionally of her arrival at a munitions factory; dressed splendidly in furs, ospreys and pearls – 'as every man-jack of them, every man, every girl, every little lad on the capstans beat on the nearest piece of iron with a hammer or spanner . . . I believe that if anyone in the factory had dared to speak of Marie Lloyd without due respect, he would have been laid out with a spanner or thrown into one of the ovens.'

Rudyard Kipling wrote a verse about her, under the misapprehension that she had lost a son at the front:

> But thou didst hide in it thy breast
> And capering took the brunt,
> Of blaze and blare, and launched the jest
> That swept next week the front.

Naomi Jacob describes how Marie was invited to an official dinner
to thank Music Hall stars for their services. (She dates it 15 March
1918, which seems curiously premature.) Marie arrived late, in the
middle of an interminable speech of self-congratulation. Her eyes
hardened and when the man had finished she stood up :

'My Lords, Ladies and Gentleman, you may not know me,' she said
with inverted modesty. 'My name is Marie Lloyd. I don't advertise.
I haven't had my photograph taken for years. I only want to say that,
apparently, in this war neither poor old Ellen Terry nor poor old
Marie Lloyd have done anything – except the gentleman who has
just spoken to you. This is not strictly correct. That's all. Thank you.'
And she walked out.

It's true that she received no recognition for her war effort, she
was excluded again from the special Royal Command in 1919 held to
show such 'appreciation', but the self-pity of her speech is so uncharacteristic, so pompous that one assumes she was troubled by
something else. Possibly the news of Dick Burge's death earlier in
the day – or a new, disastrous exploit on the part of Dillon.

Dillon had joined the army, and promptly deserted, jumping off
a moving train. When the Military Police collected him from Marie's
home, he left quietly, inviting them to have a drink on the way to
the station. He bought with Irish generosity and when they recovered
consciousness he had gone again. But he did rejoin his regiment and
even received a tiny pension of a few shillings after the war. In spite
of army service, including a spell in Mesopotamia, he seems to have
been constantly on leave (or desertion) judging by the disturbances
he caused at home. To start with, Bella and Dick Burge lived in a
house opposite, and one night Marie knocked on their door, sobbing,
and told Bella that she had come home to find Dillon in bed with
another woman.

'That's as much as I can hear about him,' said Bella, according
to Leslie Bell.

'Just you sit there and I'm going across to him.'

'Don't Bella,' said Marie, 'he'll only knock you about.'

'That's one thing he won't do, I'll promise you that.'

When Bella arrived at the house, the woman had gone but a
brandy-reeking Dillon asked her 'What the hell do you want in
here?'

'Just this Dillon. Just a few words to tell you what I think of you.'
She tore into him verbally, stepping back sharply when he made a

MARIE LLOYD

and Music Hall

move towards her, warning him 'You keep back, or somebody else will be here fast!' She finished – 'The day will come when I'll see you suffer for everything you've done to Marie. You'll finish a lot lower than you're trying to bring her.'

Another time, Marie stumbled into their house in her night-clothes, red-marks showing on her face about to turn to bruises. In a few minutes there was a hammering on the door and Dillon staggered in, but this time Dick Burge was at home and there to greet him. Picking him up, he threatened to kill Dillon if he ever laid hands on Marie again. Then he punched Dillon on the jaw, sending him sprawling down the steps.

In the light of day, Dick and Bella realized the difficult position they were in. If Dick injured Dillon, which was quite likely, he'd be in serious trouble as an ex-boxer with a criminal record. They took the drastic solution, of moving house – the same week, to Marylebone.

But the assaults on Marie continued. Dillon came regularly to the stage-door asking for money, or Marie would be phoned to collect him from the Queen's Hotel in Leicester Square, half-drunk with a woman he'd picked up, and have to settle the money that was owing. Understandably, Marie's family hated him – 'Meeting Dillon was the worst day's work she ever did' said one of them.

The death of Dick Burge took place 15 March 1918.

Ever since his early release from prison, after helping out a warder in a fight, Dick Burge had prospered. After a three-month tour of the halls, giving boxing exhibitions, he turned boxing promoter and opened the Ring at Blackfriars on 14 May 1910. The best seats were 3s and the district was rough and poor. Bella had already contributed her savings, and now she tried to win local goodwill by opening a soup kitchen in the back of the premises.

Marie, Alec and other friends in Music Hall, stood behind the coppers and ladled out bowls of soup for the ill-clad, under-fed children, with thick slices of currant bread. The line stretched for a quarter of a mile and as supplies could never satisfy the hunger the kitchen was closed after several weeks. By then the name of 'The Ring' had been established in the neighbourhood.

It proved such a success that Burge expanded. He hired Olympia for the World 'White' Heavyweight Championship and brought over Carpentier in a blaze of shrewd publicity – he won in the 6th round.

He volunteered for the army in the war and was given a special job of chaperoning a young man of title and importance who was running wild in London, seeing that he returned to his regiment in a reasonable condition on time. The young man is unnamed.

This job left him plenty of spare time and Burge went into partnership with C. B. Cochran, later the impressario of Revue. With clever bargaining, Burge got the option of Hammerstein's 'Opera House' later the 'Stoll Theatre' – for only £30,000. He was all set to become one of the biggest boxing promoters in the world when a zeppelin dropped a bomb on Piccadilly and after working through a night of pouring rain, trying to save the victims, he caught a serious chill and died three days later.

His funeral was an impressive affair for an ex-convict. There was a telegram from the King and Queen to Bella and a military funeral. Three thousand people followed the gun carriage and Alice Lloyd's husband, Tom MacNaughton, walked behind with Dick's dog Betty on a lead. The *Daily Mirror* praised Burge as: 'The greatest boxer of his time,' and said he had raised over £12,000 for war charities. 'He was a lovable and generous man, who had a host of friends.'

Forgiveness for his part in the Goudie Scandal was absolute. Towards the end of his life he was in a Turkish bath when he was sent for by the Judge who had sentenced him years earlier and recognized him through the steam. The Judge told him it would have been a very different story if the Court of Appeal had existed at the time. This must have been a poor and bitter comfort to Burge.

After the funeral, Bella refused to go to the Crematorium. Back home she made the announcement to Marie and other friends that she was going to run The Ring by herself. So Bella became the first woman boxing promoter in the country and controlled the crowds with admirable success.

18 Bernard Dillon – the Third Mr Lloyd

There were two Dillons and the one usually presented is without a saving grace. 'Ever since I was a little boy,' writes his nephew Michael, 'I dreaded reading anything about Marie Lloyd, because as sure as fate the name Dillon would appear and as usual the wicked uncle would go through the mill. Whatever people might say of him, he was a *great* jockey. He was no angel, that's for sure, but he was not the terrible person that Bella Burge, Naomi Jacob and Marie Junior make him out to be.'

Michael's mother, Alice Dillon, remembers that he sat in their living-room 'with my old white Sussex hen on his knee. He loved kippers, and he loved my children. All my life, I only heard him say "bloody" once. Of course we never knew him in spirits. He was very calm on ordinary beer.'

Michael's father, Jack Dillon, at Epsom, where Bernard brought him from Ireland when he was a child, remembers Marie: 'To us kids she was good. Every Sunday she'd bring us fancy cakes and when Bernard was in Mesopotamia, she sent us two trunks of his clothes for the boys. My children worshipped him later. He was a gentleman to them. It was only in the last years after he lost his licence that he turned out so bad.'

The good impression is confirmed by two other people who knew him well, Marie's niece and her husband, Mr and Mrs Joe Mott. Dillon was best-man at their wedding, dapper in a white shirt, black hair sleeked back, staring defensively at the camera. 'If Ben was sober,' Joe Mott told me, 'you didn't get a bad word out of him. If he was drunk he became the mad Irishman.'

'Did she love him?' I asked of Marie.

'All along.'

'Did he love her?'

'I doubt if he ever did.'

'He must have had charm?'

'At times he was like a baby, laughing like a child and playing his accordion.'

'Marie was a grand person,' said Alice Dillon, 'if only they hadn't been living in London. It was an open-house, more like a public house. There'd be seven or eight of Marie's family at the breakfast table. Always this gang, always trouble over money, always drinking – she'd drink beer in the morning as if it was tea. Bernard's mother went up there quite often, but she was a simple woman and just did not understand. I mean swear words were quite ordinary to Marie. Grannie wouldn't say much when she got back, just – "They've been at it again" '.

'Marie loved Bernard very much, but how could she show it in a house that was always full of people? Once Bernard took her to the seaside for a rest, but there were six of her gang waiting at the station to go with them. What was the pleasure in that!'

I asked her the same question : 'Did Dillon love her?' 'I truly can't make it out,' said Alice Dillon. 'He was fascinated by her. It wasn't her looks because she had no looks. He told me once – "I wish I'd been trained to marry a girl who would have had children." It's a mystery to me why he never went mad.'

Undeniably, Dillon had sex-appeal. Marie was not the only woman to fall for it, and regret. Once in Brighton, introducing him to a friend, she looked him up and down and remarked with meaning – 'This is my third husband. He's got more than the other two put together.'

Vitally, he was eighteen years younger than she was. There are problems enough when a middle-aged man marries a girl, but there is also public opinion to contend with when a woman falls for a younger man. Inexplicably, and unfairly, such a relationship creates gossip, even today. But it's not uncommon; the last husbands of two other performers, with turbulent private lives – Edith Piaf and Judy Garland – were also many years younger.

Dillon was always accused of sponging off Marie, but when he met her he had made a fortune from racing, selling an annuity for an estimated thirty to forty thousand pounds. Incredibly, they went through this together, in wild spending, and now he was merely an out-of-work jockey and the third 'Mr Lloyd'. Quick to suspect insults, he got them like the time 'Kid' Lewis told him 'I don't cater for broken-down jockeys.' Fights were inevitable; once he bit a policeman.

MARIE LLOYD and Music Hall

But the worst part of his violence, which was now a talking point of Music Hall, was the diminishing effect on Marie who began to drink more heavily than ever. At one brilliant Ball, she arrived late and started to climb slowly up the grand, curved staircase. As a waiter scurried down it balancing a giant tray of empty glasses, she swung her fist upwards and sent them smashing.

At a Charity Ball she did 'the prettiest, daintiest dance I have ever seen' wrote Naomi Jacob. Then several men burst into the room led by Dillon, and this was the first time she had ever seen Marie frightened.

'What the hell do you think you are doing here?' he asked, and struck her across the face. He was thrown out while Marie stood motionless on the table, her hand to her cheek.

Frequently, she appeared heavily-veiled to hide the bruises and swollen eyes, and sometimes had to cancel her Music Hall engagements. Her niece, Mrs Joe Mott, told me of an afternoon when she went to Oakdene, Marie's home, and was puzzled to find the doors open, but no maid or sign of life. Then she heard the faintest sound of sobbing. It came from a lean-to, 'sort of Indian-style', and there she found Marie.

'Go away, go away,' she whispered.

'And then I saw her face. If he'd been in the house I think I'd have murdered him. The maids were so terrified they'd all run away.'

It's too easy, too glib to say that Marie must have induced such violence. Perhaps there is an element of truth in this, but there's no denying that when Dillon was drunk he *was* violent.

Throughout much of this time and for many more years, he carried on an affair with a French woman called Yvonne Granville. Alice Dillon met her with Bernard at the Ostend racing season in 1923 – 'she seemed alright'. Yvonne Granville was the cause of a bitter argument during the Christmas of 1919, when several guests were staying at Oakdene. Yvonne Granville was staying in the Pink Room and Marie not only found them in bed together but was asked to join them. Dillon was surprised when she refused.

1920 was to prove the saddest year of all, though there was one moment of brightness on her fiftieth birthday in February. She was appearing at the 'Bedford' in Campden Town and the stage was filled with flowers. Music Hall veterans (and they were becoming veterans now) gave her a special bouquet with a bottle of champagne . . . swinging from the top – 'She was excited with delight and then collapsed. Poignantly, it was the only time in her life that she received a public tribute, particularly precious at this moment when public scandal was about to break over her yet again.

Early in March, Dillon overheard Marie's father and daughter and the cook gossiping about him in the kitchen. Marie Junior was running him down mercilessly, saying that her own father Percy Courtenay wasn't half as bad and why on earth didn't Marie divorce him. Dillon entered the room at this moment, infuriated by the last remark, and after telling them to keep his name out of the conversation he asked Marie Junior :

'Why don't you divorce your husband?' Turning on her, he shouted such obscenities that John Wood stepped in between saying he was like a 'madman'. At this Dillon spat in his face and knocked him down. Crying that he only wished he was twenty years younger, Wood struck back so fiercely that the cook had to go for a towel to mop up the blood from Dillon's face. As he went upstairs, John Wood said 'Good night. I forgive you, but I cannot forget.'

Dillon was charged with assault on 18 March. His solicitor asked for an adjournment because the cook was ill and would testify that it was Wood who had struck Dillon first. The prosecution agreed, saying that if the meek and gentle Dillon had indeed been hit by an old man of seventy-four, the witness should be heard.

On 30 March, the prosecution opposed a further adjournment because Dillon had broken the peace by attacking Marie a few days earlier. But the adjournment was granted. Directly underneath the report in the local paper was another, apparently separate item : 'Case dismissed. Described as independent, Bernard Dillon of Oakdene was brought before Marlborough Street charged with assaulting Yvonne Granville in the mouth with his fist in Piccadilly. She did not attend the Court and Dillon was discharged.'

At the final hearing Mary Brady, the cook, who had been at Oakdene for two years *did* testify that it was Marie's father who had been the aggressor. She said it was impossible for Dillon to have struck him first because the old man was holding him down. John Wood denied he had been the worse for drink, or excited, and said the whole story had been 'got up'. The Chairman bound Dillon over on the sum of £100 to be of good behaviour for twelve months. He said the scenes had been discreditable to all concerned and that Brady had obviously been doing her best to shield Dillon.

Even at this point, Marie refused to take sides against him. Her solicitor, Mr Groebel, appeared in Court to say that 'Marie Lloyd desired him to say personally that she had no knowledge with regard to the incident alleged to have taken place in her house, and she strongly objected to anything being said as to her connexion with the case.' It seems likely that these instructions had been given in advance. If my calculations are correct, only a few hours earlier the most vicious attack of all had taken place.

Marie was fast asleep when she was woken by Dillon climbing through the window around 3 o'clock in the morning. Still drugged with sleep, she gave a scream as he pulled her eyes open and threw liquid into them. She screamed for her maid – *'Maud! He has thrown vitriol in my eyes.'*

In fact it was spit followed by beer. Calling her every obscene name he could remember, he dragged her out of bed, struck her, and seizing hold of the water jug threw it all over her.

Unable to endure Dillon's violence any longer Marie left her home two days later. When she phoned, several days afterwards, desperate to know how things were, Dillon took the receiver from the maid and smashed it, threatening : 'If you come home I will murder you', a strange echo of Courtenay's threat thirty years earlier : 'I am going to . . . well murder you tonight.'

Marie's solicitor wrote to Dillon on 4 June :

> Dear Sir,
>   We have been consulted by Mrs Dillon with reference to your brutal and cruel conduct towards her, in consequence thereof she goes in fear of her life. We have further been consulted in reference to your being unfaithful towards her, in that you have committed yourself with divers persons in divers places.
>   Entirely without prejudice to all our client's rights, and fully reserving the same, will you please give us a call in reference thereto – here at our St Martin's Lane Office, on Wednesday next 9th at 4.30. In addition to which we must ask you at once to refrain from molesting her in any way whatsoever, as upon our instructions, your conduct is such as is causing our client serious injury to her health, mentally and physically.'

Dillon didn't bother to reply. By chance he happened to meet Mr Groebel in the street who told him that he had instructions from Marie to offer him ten pounds a week. Far from accepting this, Dillon gave a shrug, a vague answer, and moved on.

Once again Marie took a husband to court.

On 15 July she appeared with her daughter, both 'fashionably dressed', at Hendon Magistrate's Court in support of two summonses taken out against Dillon.

Huntley Jenkins appeared for Marie and said that in spite of everything she took these proceedings with the greatest possible reluctance and 'was driven as a last resource to apply to the court for protection.

'I might say that it is not putting the case too high to say that her life with this man has simply been a hell on earth. She has forgiven, as far as a woman could forgive, this man's cruel conduct and his unfaithfulness towards her. Even now, Mrs Dillon does not want this man to sink any lower than she thinks he has sunk.

'As a result of this persistent cruelty, Miss Lloyd had from time to time been incapable of fulfilling her engagements, because of black eyes and nervous prostration, that had meant a loss of several hundred pounds.'

Because of her 'nervous condition', Marie was allowed to sit when she gave evidence, telling how she was woken by a noise, as if someone was trying to break into the house, and how beer was thrown into her eyes – 'I thought it was vitriol and I screamed.' She referred to another time when he dragged her out of bed by her hair and punched her on the back and arms.

'How many times has this happened since Christmas?'

'I cannot tell you, there were so many. It has happened for years, time after time, always when he is drunk.'

Dillon defended himself, and cross-examined Marie with unconcealed bitterness.

'How many times have you been divorced?' he asked her.

Marie replied that it made no difference to the case, but it was twice. She admitted she had borrowed £1,000 from him when she had a nervous breakdown, but added :

'You know I've repaid every penny. How many thousands have you had from me since?'

Marie said she was not anxious for a divorce but would be content with a judicial separation.

More witnesses were called, including Doctor Hargreaves who confirmed he had been called to Oakdene many times during the last few years and had treated Marie for nervous collapse, bruises and black eyes. Mrs Maud Wilson, Marie's faithful maid, said : 'Many times Mr Dillon struck his wife in the face and owing to black eyes

8—MLATMH • •

she had to hide herself.' Mary Brady the cook gave evidence, this
time against Dillon, and said that in the early morning of the 27th
she heard Marie screaming – ' "Maud, he has thrown vitriol in my
eyes." Mr Dillon was using foul language and she saw the bruises
on Miss Lloyd's chest and spine.' When she mentioned the phone
call and Dillon's threat to murder Marie if she returned home,
Dillon shouted out – 'It's all lies.'

Station-Sergeant Mosley stated that the police had been called to
Oakdene on a number of occasions.

When Dillon asked for an adjournment, the magistrate refused:
'It's just as easy for you to say whether these charges are true or not.'

'There's no doubt we've had rows, but half of the things are not
true.'

'If they were only a quarter true, she'd be entitled to a separation.'

Dillon was bound over to keep the peace yet again, for twelve
months. As there was already a similar order against him, for assaulting Marie's father, Mr Lilley, the Magistrate, said this was extremely
lenient: 'It was at his wife's request they took this mild course. If
you molest her in the future, you will be sent to prison.'

The separation was granted.

19 Want to watch a Miracle?

A friend has described Marie's disintegration those last few years: 'Alone, sobbing, eating virtually nothing, completely exhausted and broken, the touch of arrogance, all the fight in her had gone. All she had left was to go out on stage and work. At least the public still wanted her and loved her.'

It's the loss of that vital 'touch of arrogance' that seems so sad. That was Dillon's crime.

Walter Barfoot was a call-boy at 'The Finsbury Park Empire' from 1915–20 and remembers that Marie was always given Dressing-Room 7 because it was on the ground floor and she was so often 'under the weather'. By the interval after the first house on Tuesday, she already needed a sub of £70 for the three shows she had played: 'Only what's due to me cock'. She had to climb wearily up the stairs to the manager's office at the back of the circle, for Coleman Hicks refused to pay out the money in front of the hangers-on that cluttered her dressing-room, along with the bottles of whisky and Guinness and the smell of fish-and-chips. There was always a crowd of women, and the odd man or two, but when they pressed Walter to come in and have a drink with them he never noticed anything 'immoral'. The only time he heard Dillon's name mentioned was her reply when her brother asked if he would be coming in that night – 'No, the bastard isn't.'

Her timing was still perfect. She'd sing four or five numbers. Her finale was usually the 'Directoire Dress', slashed towards the waist, in Cambridge blue with lots of sparklers and the cane with the diamante top.

Before the first house she would take a drink for 'Dutch Courage', but Barfoot says she was invariably the worse for drink after the Second House. Only the staff and those who knew her could really tell.

Her brother acted as her manager, but in Walter Barfoot's eyes he

MARIE LLOYD
MARIE LLOYD
and Music Hall

was a 'soak' anxious for his share of the salary like everyone else. Tips were vital to the staff of a Hall who were paid 'starvation wages'. They encouraged the superstition that when an artist failed to tip generously it meant bad luck – and they saw that it did. The orchestra in particular could wreck an act if the conductor wasn't handed his envelope to distribute among them. An American artist called Tucker, who stood sideways, dressed half as a man and half as a woman, singing baritone and soprano respectively, found himself in trouble when the orchestra persisted in playing in the wrong key for the wrong side. He had failed to tip them. Marie never made such a mistake, and handed the conductor an envelope with £10 in it every Saturday night. Later she came on stage with two £5 bags of silver to distribute among the stage-hands and electricians – 'Oh yes, you're the bugger who dropped the cloth on my head. Well, never mind.' Walter got five shillings to begin with.

He noticed it became more and more difficult to get her on stage : 'Ten minutes Miss Lloyd', then 'Five minutes Miss Lloyd', followed by a frantic 'On stage Miss Lloyd' with the answering cry of 'Oh bugger off' To make things easier, they built her a special dressing-room in the wings, concealed by scenery, but even so they had 'to watch her somewhat'. A reputation for unreliability began to spread. Finsbury Park was on the Number One Moss Circuit. Soon she was playing the Number Two Circuit and lesser halls.

Music Hall itself was in decline. The great need for it was over. The old intimacy had gone and radio had arrived. The war had changed everyone and everything. Sir Oswald Stoll forbade his artists to work for radio, and in desperation he tried anything new at 'The Coliseum' – even Annette Kellerman swimming in a large tank to Southern Syncopated Jazz.

Money was scarce and Halls were papered generously, except for Saturday nights. Yet Marie could still fill a theatre and command high salaries. In the year ending March 1918, she had two weeks' holiday and her best weekly fee was £470. The next year her biggest salary was £520 at Cardiff; and in the year ending March 1920, when she had to take three weeks off for 'rest', her earnings were £11,000 with a top weekly salary of £622. This plunged the following year, but Marie was all right so long as she was able to work, and she *had* to work – according to Alice Dillon, her sister-in-law, 'for the money she needed so desperately'. The trouble was the old extravagance, an inability to save, and the entourage of spongers.

Charles Groebel, the son of her solicitor (Groebel) remembers a visit to her dressing-room when he was a boy, with writs pinned around her mirror.

'Here's another one,' she'd say, throwing the latest to his father. 'Yet the writs were somehow paid off, and to my young eyes she was always very gracious, every inch a lady.'

Sometimes the façade slipped and revealed how frightened she was. 'I hope I shall soon be at work again, she told Chance Newton when she was ill, 'for God knows I need it. As you well know, all my oof has gone. Anyhow – I don't intend ever to send round the blinkin' hat.'

On her last tour of South Africa, there was an uncharacteristic note of self pity. 'I daren't be alone. What's the use of going on? I don't enjoy much these days.' But if she did say this and really threaten suicide – 'That's what I shall do one day. I mean it' – this was a lapse in private. Don Ross has assured me : 'Don't let anyone have the idea that Marie ever got cowed or felt sorry for herself, not in front of anyone else certainly. On the contrary, she was defiant and if offered sympathy would have been most likely to say – "What the hell has it got to do with you?"'

Don Ross showed me a photograph of Marie taken around this time. The mouth is smiling, the expression gentle, but behind the eyes there seems an infinity of sadness. In the same way, with make-up and colourful dresses, Marie presented the old flamboyance on stage, but it was different behind the scenes.

Joan Hurley was taken backstage as a child before Marie's turn : 'Mother said "Here she comes." And I looked, and said "Where?", and then I saw this old woman walking slowly towards us, holding on to the arm of her dresser. Then mother said – "You want to watch a miracle, look." I saw Marie standing there limply in the wings and then her music was played and she braced herself and walked on with the old spirit.'

The dressing-room always had a basket with lobster and champagne, but Joan Hurley never saw her eat.

No longer was Marie late at the halls, after a day at the races. Now she arrived early to play interminable games of patience. Sometimes her late entrance was unavoidable, while she was massaged in the wings for her rheumatism or given an injection. But the delay still brought the audience to the 'tiptoe of impatient eagerness' as one critic recorded, and she was skilful enough to exploit her mistakes.

'The poor conductor listening for his cue among the patter, loses himself, finds himself again and picks up the melody; while Marie Lloyd supremely sure of herself and disdainful of other accompanists, carries on with a total disregard of them.'

In April 1922, she collapsed at Cardiff in her dressing-room after singing *The Cosmopolitan Girl*, the only number she could manage. The curtain rose on another performer. Her last appearance in the North was at the 'Gateshead Empire'.

Her voice was now so weak that the other artists on the bill helped her out by singing along with her.

In August 1922, she staged something of a 'come-back', at least a newspaper heading reads 'Marie Lloyd returns in Triumph', but the review suggests that already she belonged to another age : 'The daughters and nieces join with perfunctory hand-clapping in the vociferous cheers of the gallery. And once more you start wondering exactly how she strikes the new generation of theatre-goers.'

A month later, the audience were so shocked by her appearance that they gasped aloud. When they kept on cheering at the end, she came back on stage in a simple, pink dressing-gown and made a little speech : 'I hope I may, without bigotry, allude to my past triumphs. When I was first a star, I stood here and sang a song that everyone sang, and nobody said it was naughty. Sing it with me now.' And the audience sang with her, indeed for her, the jaunty words of *Oh, Mr Porter*.

By now, says Alice Dillon, 'her mind had almost gone'. The projection of her singing voice was so feeble that one particular girl would stand in the wings and sing the songs as loudly as she could – a macabre version of modern mime. The audiences could not have been fooled, but they understood.

The end came a few weeks' later at Edmonton. Marie was top of an indifferent Bill, as if Music Hall was dying with her. On the Tuesday she was so ill that the doctor was called to her home and ordered Marie to stay there. But for her, there was no choice. She arrived at her dressing-room early and was massaged into a semblance of life. Her make-up was applied so heavily that it looked grotesque, at close quarters. She was helped, almost lifted into her costume, but she managed to finish her turn for the First House and then she collapsed. She lay prone in the dressing-room while they whispered around her, wondering what to do, persuading her to go home. Then she heard a strange, clumping sound that grew into thunder and recognized the familiar stamp of the gallerites as they climbed upwards to the Gods on the stairs above the room.

'They're coming to see *me*!' she said, with a spark of the old arrogance.

She waited listlessly in the wings, holding on to the scenery. Then came that inimitable intro music, bright and tantalizing as ever, and suddenly there was Marie. Her last song was one of those remarkable 'character' numbers that distinguished the climax of her career: *It's a Bit of a Ruin that Cromwell Knocked About a Bit*. Marie appeared as a worn-out old dear, scrummaging through her handbag for a drop of gin. With lines like 'a relic from a byegone age' – it was agonizingly appropriate.

'Hold on,' she said, opening her bag. 'Half a mo, I've come over funny. Here, 'aint you ever been like it. Well, if you 'aint I must have copped the lot. It's a sort of a feeling that says to you – Look old girl, it's time you had one. And that reminds me, I've got a little drop of you-know-what which does we-know-how in here . . . I shan't detain you a moment, while I have a little search for it.' Panic in her eyes, as the battered bag was left swinging open. 'Hullo – it's gone Would you believe it, when I came out of my house this morning I had a nice little drop of gin in here. But you can see for yourself, can't you? Bottle, cork and all gone. You know what's happened to me? I've been buzzed. That's what comes from sitting in the long grass with a stranger. I'm the unluckiest girl in the world – Sooki Hardcastle; it doesn't matter what I go out with, I'm bound to go home without it.'

Then she began to sing, or speak, this extraordinary song:

> I'm very fond of ruins, and ruins I like to scan
> And when you talk of ruins,
> Why you should see my old man

In keeping with the character, she staggered, and the audience laughed not realizing she was ill.

> . . . in the gay old days, there must have been some doings
> No wonder that the poor old Abbey went to ruins . . .

She staggered, uncontrollably, and the audience roared. Then she fell and the curtain was lowered while the audience continued to laugh and cheer. When the curtain rose again the stage was empty, and the audience was still unaware that the curtain had fallen on 'Our Marie' for the last time.

When she died, three days later, on 7 October 1922, the Bills were already going up at 'The Alhambra'

Next Week, welcome return of Marie Lloyd

20 As Big as Waterloo Station

The ultimate in the myth of Marie came with her death – that she died of a 'broken heart'. A close, surviving relative assured me that the doctor could find nothing wrong with her – 'the only explanation was a broken heart'. Macqueen Pope, less forgivably, wrote : 'The complaint was incurable, some might call it heartbreak.'

Conversely, a wild rumour whispered that she died of syphillis, which she caught from Dillon. I have been assured that she attended the Lydia Ward of St Thomas' Hospital for treatment, but there is no evidence of this.

The Death Certificate, signed by the doctor who had treated her over the years, Dr Hargreaves, states : Nitral Regurgitation – 14 months; Nephritis (an inflammation of the kidneys) 14 months; and Uraemic Coma – 3 days.

It's always been claimed that she died in the arms of her sister Rosie, but in fact it was Dillon who was with her at the last moment. The address – 37 Woodstock Road, Golders Green, is given as his residence and also the place where Marie died.

A wave of emotion, tinged with remorse, swept over England.

T. S. Eliot was moved to write : 'Although I have always admired the genius of Marie Lloyd I do not think that I always appreciated its uniqueness; I certainly did not realize that her death would strike me as the important event it was. Marie Lloyd was the greatest Music Hall artist of her time in England : she was also the most popular.'

James Agate remembered the last little speech at 'The Alhambra' when she spoke of her past triumphs without, she hoped, 'bigotry', 'Poor soul,' he wrote, 'it is we who should be asked to be delivered from that vice. She broadened life and showed it not as a mean affair of refusal and restraint, but as a boon to be lustily enjoyed. She redeemed us from virtue too strait-laced, and her great heart cracked too soon.'

He overheard a party of bookmakers returning from Kempton Races – 'She had a heart had Marie,' said one, tearfully.

'The size of Waterloo Station,' replied another.

Too late, the tributes flowed. '. . . the world seems colder and emptier. The death of a great laughter-maker seems to many like the end of laughter' (*The Manchester Guardian*). *The Stage* made the vital observation : 'She was as much part and parcel of her time as Dickens and Thackeray.'

George Godwin, a free-lance journalist who was asked to 'ghost' Marie's life story, told me that he got most of his material from her sister Alice. 'Just before I left, Alice said – "Would you like to see her?" I find no pleasure in contemplating death, but I felt I must, out of courtesy, assent. Marie was in the open coffin in the next room. In death, her face was composed but one of her prominent front teeth was missing, which gave her face a pathetic appearance. Then her sister said – "Dillon knocked that tooth out" '. A poignant reminder of the famous smile and the front teeth which Agate compared to 'those of a jovial horse'.

The Will was read while Dillon was expelled to the kitchen – the family would have nothing to do with him – and if he expected any share of the money he was disappointed. Marie left £300 to her brother Johnny, £100 to Maud, the faithful maid to whom she had screamed on the night when Dillon threw liquid in her eyes. All the rest was to be invested for Marie Junior who would receive the interest until her death, when the rest would go to Hoxton Charities. Altogether, she left about £7,000.

Her funeral was one of those rare occasions when all London shares the same sense of loss. Pubs were draped in black crepe and between fifty to a hundred thousand people held up the endless procession. In mourning the death of Marie, they mourned Music Hall as well.

First came twelve cars laden with flowers – a vast model of a stage from her agent, with red-roses before the curtain; a replica of a bird-cage, open, with the linnet gone; posies from the flower sellers of Piccadilly; seven hearts from the seven Lloyd sisters; a horseshoe of white chrysanthemums from her 'Jockey Pals'; flowers from Bella and 'The Ring'; wreaths from every Music Hall star, including one from Clarice Mayne to 'The greatest woman of our time'. There was even a wreath from Sir Oswald Stoll. A simple bunch of flowers lay at the foot of the coffin, from her parents.

On top of the hearse lay the long ebony cane with the diamante top that she used in the song about the Directoire Dress. Behind the hearse came her own car, the blinds drawn though people glimpsed a rug thrown over the empty seat much as she must have left it.

Then the long calvalcade of mourners and one car with the solitary, white-faced widower Bernard Dillon.

The crowd groaned as he passed by.

1935 – November 22 : Bernard Dillon charged and acquitted of assaulting Mrs Welford and stealing £3 from her.

'I am suggesting to you,' said Mr Cloutman in cross-examination, 'that you are nothing more or less than a pot-house blackguard.'

'It is very wrong of you to say that,' Dillon replied, 'I am proud of my record.' He said he was a racing tipster and lived with Mrs Welford in Westbourne Grove.

1939 – 41 : Dillon took a job in Africa House as a night porter. His brother says – 'He still had the broad shoulders, but the rest had gone.'

1941 – May 6 : Bernard Dillon dies at St Mary Abbots Hospital, Paddington. 'The Widow of the deceased, Mrs Josephine Dillon was present at the death.'

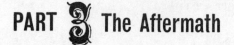

PART **3** The Aftermath

21 The Old Met

My own involvement with Marie Lloyd and Music Hall began with the Metropolitan in the Edgware Road. I never saw Marie, except in my mind's eye, and I never knew Music Hall in its heyday, but by chance I became involved with its death.

The old 'Met', as it was affectionately known, was hardly noticeable in the growing seediness of the district. But inside it was huge and brown with hints of vanished opulence. Cherubs abounded and plaster caryatides supported the baroque boxes. Also, and all-important, there was a large mahogany bar with a glass front where you could watch the artists, hear them through a loud-speaker, and drink and gossip at the same time. I am sure this was part of the flavour of the old Music Hall – that many people came to watch one or two turns only and spend the rest of the time eating and drinking and ogling along the Promenade.

I was working for the television programme *This Week* when I heard that the 'Met' was going to be demolished, in the spring of 1957, and I thought this could make an interesting programme. I knew nothing of Music Hall apart from one visit to 'Collins' at Islington Green where the entertainment was so awful it was almost appealing.

Filming at the 'Met', I began to realize what Music Hall was all about. We filmed the famous 'Chocolate Coloured Coon, G. H. Elliott, who was in his mid-seventies. He sang *Lily of Laguna* one of the immortal songs of Music Hall, which he was quick to acknowledge had originated with an earlier 'Coon' performer Eugene Stratton.

The Black-and-White Minstrels may sing-along with rather forced bonhomie, but Elliott was the last true 'Coon' performer. This popular vogue of Music Hall could hardly survive our racialism, with reference to 'palpitating niggers' and 'Mr Bones'. For innocence was the supreme quality of the Minstrels, with such favourite jokes as :

Magistrate : Are yo' guilty or not guilty.
Prisoner : Not guilty, jedge.
Magistrate : Then what the Dickens yo' doin' here – wastin' our time?

Several of the most exhuberant Music Hall songs came from the Minstrel : *Ta-Ra-Ra-Boom-De-Ay* and *Bill Bailey*, both American, but *Laguna* and Elliott's own favourite *I used to sigh for the silvery moon* were the gentle counterpart. Leslie Stuart composed many of the best love ballads and Colin Macinnes recounts a moment when he appeared at the 'Palladium' in 1930, alone with a piano. Without any explanation Stuart sat down and played such numbers as *Laguna* and *Little Dolly Daydream*. As it dawned on the audience that he had written them all, and was still alive, they interrupted him with a spontaneous ovation. He was born in Southport in 1864 and his real name was Thomas Barrett. Because he arranged classical concerts – bringing Paderewski to Manchester, he used the pseudonym of Stuart for his popular songs.

Elliott was born in Rochdale in 1883 and moved to America with his parents. At the age of nine he joined his first minstrel show and at the age of eleven made his first gramophone record on one of the old cylinders of the Edison Recording Company. Back in England he was billed as 'Master George Elliott – the Wonderful Boy Soprano'.

When Elliott was twenty, he topped the bill for the first time, at 'The Parthenon Music Hall' in Liverpool.

His world was over when I saw him. He described the end of the Music Halls as 'a tragedy to the nation'. As the orchestra played the beautiful introduction to *Laguna* – and so often in the old songs the verse has an enchanting delicacy compared to the better-known chorus – I sensed the *charm* of Music Hall. He sang the words as if he believed them, with none of that brittle breeziness of the imitations of today.

His voice quavered; he could no longer capture that little yodel in the middle of the song, and I wished he wouldn't try; and the soft-shoe shuffle between the words was a shadow of a past performance, but his dignity was absolute as he doffed his hat at the end and bowed to the audience. Little wonder that the ladies fell for him.

One of the most amazing qualities of the Music Hall artists was their stamina. Far from being worn out, they seemed unable to stop.

Elliott was one of the last veterans to tour with *Thanks for the Memory*. This had been brought in to the 'Palladium' as a stop-gap but proved a surprising success in its own right even though some of the artists had to be replaced as they died off. The tour reintroduced two of the great comediennes of the century – Nellie Wallace and Lily Morris who took her place. At a time when the stage was considered wicked, it's interesting that so many – if not most – of the great Music Hall stars were women.

The man responsible for *Thanks for the Memory* was Don Ross, the last impresario of Music Hall. He was married to Gertie Gitana and lived in a house called 'Neldean', after *Nellie Dean* the song she made famous.

Don Ross took part in the programme at the 'Met', scorning the standards of the present in telling of the star quality of the past and how the old artists always made an 'entrance'.

'We were taught not to expect to get anywhere in our profession unless we worked hard and practised hard, and also to have a great respect for the public ... they were the masters. Of course artists did earn very big salaries, but they were never in a position to earn those salaries unless they could fill a theatre. In these days the most extraordinary people earn extraordinary salaries, but they do not even fill a theatre.' It was Ross who told me of Ida Barr and advised me to see her.

I had never heard of her. She lived in a dreadful tenement block that tried to hide itself behind Charing Cross Road. The 'buildings' had an institutional air – or rather airlessness about them, but her flat was instantly recognizable as the only one of the several hundred which made any gesture of defiance. A large china gnome swung on the balcony and a few plants in pots struggled for the few seconds' sunlight that reached them in the day. Inside, the two cramped rooms crowded with bric-a-brac had the gaiety of a country cottage. She was living on National Assistance – and she was happy.

22 Ida Barr

Ida Barr was born in London's Albany Street Barracks in 1882 as Maud Barlow: 'I weighed fourteen pounds and my mother said I kicked my way into the world. I've been kicking ever since.' Her father was a Sergeant Major in the Life Guards with strong views on the conduct of young ladies and Ida in particular. Once she went with another girl to Southend where they were picked up by two young men. One presented Ida with his walking stick and back home her father demanded to know where she got it. Expecting this, she replied promptly that she found it floating in the sea. Her father thought this over for a moment, removed the horse-whip that hung on the wall, and told her to bend over. After several agonizing strokes, he stopped: 'And now go upstairs and try floating your ebony cane in the bath.'

'I was stage mad but he thought the stage was wicked.' When Ida was fifteen she ran away to Ireland to join the chorus of a pantomime under the name of 'Maud Laverne', which she thought was 'posh', like Marie with 'Bella Delmere'. She weighed thirteen stone, seven pounds – 'They liked a lot of woman in those days' – and a photograph the following year, with a vast, embroidered shamrock on her bust shows that she was exquisite.

She returned to London to play *The Sultan of Morocco* for £2 10s a week at 'The Pavilion', Whitechapel: 'I had to black myself all over and it ruined my underclothes. But they never paid me a penny more.'

In 1910 she ran off again, this time to America, away from her husband Gus Harris a comedian billed as 'The only Yiddisher Scotsman in the Irish Fusiliers'. Jealous of Ida's popularity, the explosion came when the management announced they had placed her at the top of the bill and himself at the bottom. 'That's all right,' said Ida tactfully, 'they can put me at the bottom and you at the top.' The manager explained brutally that it was Ida the public came to see, and Harris walked out of the theatre.

Ida sailed to New York where the going was tough, but in the best tradition she persevered and saw her name in lights in Los Angeles in 1912. She returned to England with a new dance craze, ragtime, and a song she helped make famous: 'Everybody's Doing It Now'.

In a 'Gigantic Race-Week Programme' in August, at the 'Hippo-drome', Stockton-on-Tees, Ida headed the bill as 'The Actress Vocalist', above the other main attraction: '*Mascot* – The Best Educated Horse in the World.' Other billings described her as 'Naughty but Nice' and 'Red-headed but clever'.

Ida brought over another song and made this her own: *Oh, You Beautiful Doll*. She started confidentially, almost beckoning the audience:

> Honey dear,
> Listen here,
> Just turn out the light
> And then come over here.
> Nestle close up to my side
> My heart's afire
> With love's desire.
>
> In my arms, rest complete
> I never knew that love
> Could ever be so sweet
> Till I met you
> Some time ago
> So now you know
> I love you so . . .

into the resounding chorus of *Oh, You Beautiful Doll*! She sang the words with total conviction, as a love-song, and hated the jaunty versions we hear today.

Ida topped 'The Lyceum' and this was the height of her success. She begged one admirer not to send her any more bouquets: 'I hate to see them flowers all cut and tied in wire. They've got feelings, just like us!' That night a basket of lillies of the valley arrived at the theatre. They were growing in their own soil and it took four men to lift them on to the stage.

Soon she was off again, to South Africa and Australia – with a new song *STOP, STOP, STOP*, '. . . don't you *dare* to stop, come over

and love me some more'. She triumphed, but she turned down the
offers from the Managements who asked her to stay : 'They all knew
I was in love with a feller in South Africa; I'd have gone there if I'd
had to travel by cattle-boat.' So they gave her a farewell presentation
of a carved boomerang, with the engraved plaque

'To Miss Ida Barr. Congratulating her upon her wonderful success
socially and artistically in Australia.'

'And what happened to the man in South Africa?' I asked her.
'He died.' For just a moment the big eyes saddened. 'Oh well,' she
said with a shrug, 'I was never lucky in love.' The saucy smile
returned. 'In those days it was the old ones who were after me, now
it seems to be the young fellows like yourself.'
A rare moment when I heard her indulge in regret was when she
told me of the decline of Music Hall, and her own appeal with it.
'If only I'd had someone behind me,' she said, for without a shrewd
manager or husband, Ida was never the household name nor the
rich woman she deserved to be. Red-headed but not clever enough,
she was taken advantage of, by agents and Management. Generosity
was one of her weaknesses – if one can ever call it that. The door-
man of a Hall, long demolished, told me how she sent out money to
the barefoot children who clustered round the stage-door. At that
time she was travelling by brougham between three theatres a night,
giving a total of five performances. But she was unable to save, like
so many of them.
Most of the people I spoke to at this time, bathed Music Hall in a
rosy glow of nostalgia. Everyone was 'a lovely artiste' and 'a darling
person', though I noticed that when *I* praised one of their rivals
they were quick to correct me – 'Of course that wasn't really her
song, she pinched it from so-and-so' or 'a nice little performer, but
never a headliner'. Ida was free of such malice, and hugely sentimental, but she was a realist. She liked to be earthy, telling stories
against herself like the two sailors who saw her pushing her way past
the queue into the Stage Door.
'That's Ida Barr', exclaimed one of the sailors.
'Which one?' said the other.
'The big fat one with red hair.'
'Ida Barr. She could hide a bleeding pub.'
Another story concerned Houdini with whom she toured the North

of England : 'A real nice feller. He was very religious, did you know? always went to sleep in his cap after saying his prayers.'

The star seldom closed the bill, and the great Houdini preceded Ida who was the last turn. One night, to her dismay, she was given 'the bird' for the first time in her life. She continued to sing, but the whispers and giggles spread through the theatre until the whole audience was shaking with uncontrollable laughter. Unable to imagine what was wrong, Ida finished bravely with tears in her eyes.

Unknown to her, Houdini's water-tank in which he had just performed some miracle of escapology, had sprung a leak. As she sang in front of the curtain, a trickle ran slowly between her legs. 'The audience thought I'd wet my drawers. Mr Houdini was furious. He told the manager he'd never let me be insulted like that again and from that night he insisted in going on last.'

But it was Marie Lloyd in particular who came down to earth in talks with Ida. The tinsel began to fall and at once she became a real person, which she had never seemed before.

Though they were friends, Marie was jealous of Ida, with suspicions that Dillon fancied her. According to Ida, this was untrue. She *was* having an affair with one of the race-horse trainers, 'Widge' Fallon, and Dick Burge tried to seduce her once in the Charing Cross Hotel but hadn't succeeded, Ida added rather wistfully.

Ida admired Marie 'She was the greatest, God bless her' but refused to join the entourage of women who alway surrounded her. 'They encouraged her to drink. They said "you ought to eat something Marie"; why didn't they put some nice tit-bit down in front of her?'

Ida was the first person with a good word for Dillon : 'People say he lived off her; they forget they ran through his money first. If she threw things at him – well, you can't expect a man to take that.' After Marie's funeral, when Dillon was not allowed in the front-room with the sisters, Ida stayed with him in the kitchen until he realized he wasn't in the will, took his hat and left. Her stories of Dillon and their drunkenness intrigued me, for otherwise I faced a conspiracy of respectability – even from Bella Burge.

After the programme on the 'Met', which had a sudden reprieve, I made two more television programmes on the Music Hall in a series called *Farson's Guide to the British*. It was then that I met the radiant Marie Kendall, and the not so radiant Bella Burge.

Bella was either naturally phlegmatic, or more likely, to borrow a phrase from *Mrs Shufflewick,* 'the gin and tonic had fogged the brain'.

'Was Marie ever temperamental behind the scenes?' I asked her.

'No, never.'

'No faults?'

'No.'

'Then she must have been a unique human being.'

'There weren't any faults at all,' she continued impassively. 'She was just natural in everything, in her home, in everything she did. You'd never have thought her a genius like she was.'

'You would say she had genius?'

'She was a genius in every way. I mean, she never rehearsed anything. She used to have a song, just a bit of paper, go to bed, get it in her head overnight. Just the piano would be played for her to get the tune of it and she'd walk on to the stage, and you never knew what she was going to do.'

'Did she have a great sense of humour?'

'Yes, wonderful, wonderful. She always saw the humorous side of everything.'

'Do you mean to say she had no human failings at all?'

'No. She loved her home and was very domesticated. She was a good mother. She could cook a lunch, she . . .' I interrupted her :

'You make her sound slightly dull,' I smiled.

'Dull?' Bella thought this over, unsmilingly. 'Well, I think geniuses *are* dull,' she said with a scowl.

At the time, in my ignorance, I thought this quite amusing. But how could Bella have said such things? More than anyone, she knew of Marie's temper, the scandals and disasters. Had she forgotten the times she had to comfort Marie after Dillon had beaten her up? Had Bella, in perpetuating the myth, come to believe it herself? Or didn't she know or care what she was saying?

When I asked about the time they sailed to New York, Bella said flatly that Marie didn't realize Dillon was aboard.

'Was this a scandal at the time?' I asked innocently.

'No it wasn't a scandal, but you know what the New York papers are, I don't need to tell you,' she chortled.

'And did that shock her?'

'No she didn't seem to mind . . .' she said unbelievingly.

Only later did I realize that I had been speaking to an astonishingly brave woman, and a considerable personality – the first boxing promoter in England. There was not a glimpse of it left.

In contrast, Marie Kendall at the age of ninety had an elegance and vivacity that it made it easy to understand her popularity. She started at the age of eight and appeared in 'Collins' for the first time seventy-seven years earlier. 'I was singing *A Little Yankee Masher* and I was supposed to smoke a cigarette – "I'm a little Yankee masher and a little la-di-dah" and my beloved mother would say "walk along darling, show your teeth" – "I'll jog along quite happily, as I puff my big cigar.'"

Her favourite song had charm, but now seems sentimental:

> Just like the ivy on the old garden wall
> Clinging so tightly, what e'er may befall
> And as you grow older, I'll be constant and true
> And just like the ivy, I'll cling to you.

When she was arrested in 1907 during the Music Hall Strike, she sang this at the top of her voice as she was taken to the police station, followed by supporters. 'I've also had the very great honour of singing it to the beloved Queen Mary on one, two, three occasions,' she told me. 'I appeared at the first Command in 1912 and I'm very proud to tell you that in 1932 at the Royal Command at the "Palladium", I was the last turn after a very wonderful programme.'

As for her own favourite performer: 'Marie Lloyd. I revere her memory and I had a sincere affection for her because I knew the woman she was, kind in every possible shape and form. Anyone in need who approached Marie Lloyd for help, never went away unless she did her very best for them.'

She remembered the Chairman at 'Collins' calling the Gallery to order; and the bar at the back of the stalls where they had tables for the men to put their drinks.

More details were recalled by another veteran on our programme, Albert Le Fre, who said that almond cakes and oranges were sold in the halls around Hoxton and trotter bones were thrown at artists who got the bird, or carefully pitched into the euphonium in the orchestra. 'You could go into the balcony for 6d and that entitled you to 4d worth of refreshments in the shape of a 2d cigar and a glass of beer.' As for the audience he told me that many women used to come barefoot, but that one proprietor in Liverpool 'wanted to go one better and had a notice over the pay-box to say that ladies were not admitted without shoes and stockings. And at the 'Star' Bermondsey, they would not admit anybody in the stalls unless they had a collar and tie.

Albert Le Fre was one of three brothers with an acrobatic act at a salary of £12 a week between them and with all their own expenses to pay. 'We managed all right. Things were very cheap in those days, you know. Ten shillings a week for digs, fourteen if we wanted to be a bit extravagant. We all had more fun then, more like a family.'

Demolition still threatened the 'Met', but like a reluctant prima-donna, the last night was constantly postponed. The shows became more tawdry, with strip and wrestling and Irish nights, to the distress of Maudie who had been a barmaid there for fifty years and spoke nostalgically of the broughams and top-hats: 'I only served champagne, brandy and whisky soda in those days . . . now it's beer.'

One afternoon I hired the 'Met' to make a record. This was brash enthusiasm, but by now I was fascinated by Music Hall and wanted to make a record of it in every sense. I raised £600 from friends, who are fewer, poorer and wiser now, and with the help of a colourful music publisher called Eddie Rogers I hired the stage and the old 'Met' orchestra with their Musical Director Ivan Dozin.

A skilful recording-mixer makes it sound as if it was a night of standing-room-only. In fact it was a cold afternoon with some very old old-age pensioners and a coachload of Chelsea Pensioners in their scarlet uniforms. As they hobbled down to the front two rows, someone warned me that I hadn't insured them and would have to pay fearful damages if there was an accident. Hastily I started to introduce the artists, and I wince today when I hear my bright little comments: '. . . and tonight at the age of eighty-five he is still going strong having thankfully recovered from the operation in which he lost his leg. He is *still* whistling his signature tune – Albert Whelan!'

Fortunately, Whelan rose above the occasion and gave a surprisingly vigorous rendering of the number he made famous in the First World War – *The Preacher and the Bear*. It was extraordinary to think he'd entertained miners in the gold rush at Coolgardie in the last century; even more so when I visited the place a few years later and found it a ghost town. Whelan had come from Melbourne and made his début in London as a 'scare-crow' dancer. Later he became famous for his signature tune which he whistled as he removed his cloak, hat and gloves. In his book on *The Northern Music Hall*, G. J. Mellor tells how Oswald Stoll refused to allow him more than eight minutes for his act at 'The Coliseum'. Whelan took his revenge by walking on leisurely, and disrobing his immaculate white gloves, topper, scarf and overcoat, and then putting them all on again – whistling all the time – in eight minutes exactly.

Ida Barr arrived with earrings the size of eggs saying; 'I know they're old-fashioned, but I wore them on the stage fifty years ago, and I'm going to wear 'em now.'

G. H. Elliott sang *I used to sigh for the Silvery Moon*, which he had performed for the first time at the 'Hackney Empire' in 1908. Billy Danvers, who was christened 'William Mikado Danvers' because he was born in Liverpool while his father was playing the Mikado, was the comic in the old tradition : 'Three men – (laugh) – three men stood in a pub having a drink, you know, all boasting about their wives – it's very seldom you find a man boasting about his wife, especially when she's not there. One said "My wife has *the* most beeootiful eyes in the world, they're pale blue." The other said "That's nothing. My wife's got lovely eyes as well, they're grey eyes." So they turned to the third one and said "Tom, what's the colour of your wife's eyes?" "I don't know. I've not noticed. I should have done. I've been married long enough." And it worried him. So he went home but he couldn't find her in the slavery – (laugh) the kitchen, so he went into the 'lee-ounge' and there she was sat on the settee in her dressing-gown reading, so he went straight up to her, looked right into her face, and said : "BROWN" – and a feller got up from behind the settee and said, "How did you know I was here?"

Marie Lloyd Junior represented her mother, as always, with a boisterous version of : *It's a bit of a ruin that Cromwell knocked about a bit*. A superb piece of mimicry which made me long for the original, and the heart that was lacking. She told a reporter from the *Daily Mail* : 'When *we* have gone, you can really say that Music Hall has gone.'

Marie Junior had brought Bella Burge, who seemed even more taciturn than before. If you know the moment and listen carefully, you can detect a slight thud as I make one of my awful introductions. This was when Bella Burge who had not only found but consumed an entire bottle of gin, staggered on to the stage, took hold of the curtain and slid slowly to the floor. Then, like Hamlet, she was carried off unconscious. It made the afternoon for the Chelsea Pensioners.

The LP – which is simply called MUSIC HALL – included Hetty King the last of the Male Impersonators.

23 Hetty King - and the art of the Male Impersonator

Today, pubs, clubs and even theatres abound with female impersonators. At the turn of the century the vogue was the 'male impersonator'.

Sorting through a collection of sheet music, I found such favourites as: Bessie Bonehill *The British Tar*, who is reported to have 'died' young in 1902; Millie Hylton with the *Rowdy Dowdy Boys*, whose sister took the surprising stage name of Lydia Flopp. There was Fanny Robina *King of the Boys*; Constance Moxon with *George Dear*; and Nelly Power with *Such a Mash*, whose straight number *The Boy in the Gallery* was pinched by Marie Lloyd who turned it into a triumph of her own.

And of course there was Vesta Tilley. Born in 1864, the second of a family of thirteen, she was christened Matilda, like Marie. Using her father's stage name of Ball, she started her career in Nottingham as Matilda Ball when she was only four years old. The next year she wore boy's clothes and continued as a male impersonator for the rest of her life. She came to London when she was ten as 'The great little Tilley': 'and there was much speculation among my audiences as to whether I was a boy or a girl.' The manager suggested billing her as 'Lady Tilley' to end the confusion, but she disliked this and drew the name of Vesta out of a hat.

She became known as 'The London Idol' and her career lasted almost as long as Music Hall itself.

Gus Rogers, of Nathans, who used to prepare Vesta Tilley's wigs, was one of the few people I could find who remembered her, and he did so with admiration: 'Oh what a lovely lady – so kind. She wasn't like the other artists who'd pop out for a drink, *she* wouldn't. She'd go home or to a party of her own standard.'

Thinking how much Marie must have disliked her, I asked him if he thought Tilley was the finer artist of the two.

'They weren't in the same world. Tilley attracted *all* the classes

Ida Barr in costume at the age of sixteen

(Above) *Covers of songs made famous by male impersonators.*
(Right) *Miss Hetty King dressed as a sailor, with pipe, parrot and bird cage. A photograph signed to the author.*

Kind thoughts
Good wishes
Hetty King

Two photographs of G. H. Elliott, as a young man and in middle age, both signed to the author.

In the profession she was considered much higher than Marie Lloyd; she was IT.'

Don Ross disagreed. 'Vesta Tilley is always held up as the greatest but I do not agree with that and I saw her many, many times. She had great charm and personality but if you were looking for a woman who really made you feel she was a man, which I presume is the ultimate in male impersonation, then I think Hetty King was much finer. Neat, precise, clean, she carried the character acting side to the greatest extent.

'Yet Ella Shields (an American) was my favourite, not emphasizing the masculinity of her males but giving them great charm. The uniforms and kilts and clergyman's clothes were not for Ella.'

Ella Shields can be seen on film, performing a slightly sinister number called *They don't think I'm all there*. With her strong American accent and a hollow chuckle as she taps her head, it is hard to see the 'charm' that Don Ross refers to. 'Quite horrid,' exclaimed the woman in the next seat to me.

But it's easy to imagine her impact in another, very different number : *Burlington Bertie from Bow*, written and composed by her husband William Hargreaves. This was a sequel to an earlier number of Vesta Tilley's, a plain *Burlington Bertie* in which she was a genuine toff who rose at ten-thirty and toddled along to the Strand. In Hargreaves' version, poor Bertie has taken a tumble and now lives in Bow. Threadbare but proud, he remembers the past in a splendid sequence of name-dropping :

> I'm Bert, P'raps you've heard of me,
> Bert . . . you've had word of me,
> Jogging along, hearty and strong, living on plates of fresh
> air.
> I dress up in fashion, and when I'm feeling depressed,
> I shave from my cuff all the whiskers and fluff, stick my
> hat on
> And toddle up West.
>
> I'm Burlington Bertie,
> I rise at ten-thirty and saunter along like a toff,
> I walk down the Strand with my gloves on my hand,
> Then I walk down again with them off,
> I'm all airs and graces, correct easy paces,

Without food so long I've forgot where my face is –
I'm Bert, Bert, I haven't a shirt, but my people are well off,
    you know
Nearly ev'ry one knows me, from Smith to Lord Roseberry
I'm Burlington Bertie from Bow.

I'm Burlington Bertie,
I rise at ten-thirty
And reach Kempton Park about three,
I stand by the rail, when a horse is for sale
And you ought to see Wooton watch me,
I lean on some awning, while Lord Derby's yawning,
Then he bids 'Two Thousand', and I bid 'good morning',
I'm Bert . . .

It's a long number, with no repetition apart from Bertie rising at
ten-thirty. The final verse and chorus claims a delightful acquaint-
ance, indeed familiarity with the Royal Family, always popular with
Music Hall audiences :

My pose, tho' ironical
Shows that my monocle
Holds up my face, keeps it in place, stops it from slipping
    away,
Cigars I smoke thousands, I usually deal in the Strand,
But you've got to take care, when you're getting them there
Or some idiot might stand on your hand.

I'm Burlington Bertie,
I rise at ten-thirty
Then Buckingham Palace I view;
I stand in the yard while they're changing the guard,
And the King shouts across – 'Toodle-oo',
The Prince of Wales' brother, along with some other,
Slaps me on the back, and says 'come and see mother.'
I'm Bert, Bert and Royalty's hurt, when they ask me to
    dine I say 'No !'
I've just had a Banana with Lady Diana,
I'm Burlington Bertie from Bow'

This is surely one of the greatest songs of Music Hall — a monument to snobbery, which must have amused the audience, with lyrics that are genuinely witty. There's an air of tragedy as well, and Colin Macinnes records that 'the audience seemed to get rather uneasy' as Ella Shields performed it, prowling about the stage as late as the 1940s. Plainly, she was not a comfortable personality.

When she came over from America for the first time, she was known as a 'Coon shouter' — a white artist who sang Negro songs in ragtime style, and she told Colin Macinnes of her meeting with Marie Lloyd in the dressing-room of the 'Tivoli': 'And I remember what she said. "So you're the great coon shouter. You don't look like a coon shouter. You know what you look like? You look like a dainty Maid of Albion." And I must confess my ignorance — I didn't know what the word Albion meant. And it shows you the loveliness of the woman — in her nature. I was the newcomer and stranger among them, and she said: "Why, you're just a blooming lovely English girl!"'

When I spoke to Hetty King, several years after our afternoon at the 'Met', she voiced her displeasure at having been included among lesser artists. I didn't improve matters when I started our discussion with the statement: 'I believe there have been only three great male impersonators — Vesta Tilley, Ella Shields and Hetty King.'

'No!' she thundered. 'Vesta Tilley, Hetty King, and *then little Miss Shields*.' She picked up the last few words distastefully and let them drop. Speaking of herself in the third person, she continued: 'Naturally smaller fry came along, but I didn't see them. A star would never embarrass a lesser one. Let me tell you something else — it does not mean a woman putting on trousers; if it did, practically every woman in the street would be a male impersonator. It's a great art. Hetty King is the only *true* male impersonator.'

Why did the male impersonator have such popularity, when there was only one famous female impersonator (apart from the pantomime 'Dames') — Bert Erroll? I mentioned the suggestion that the appeal was sensual, at a time when women's clothes were so voluminous that Edwardian gentlemen found it exciting to see girls in tight-fitting uniforms. Don Ross had agreed with this: 'Obviously there was a strong sex angle. After all, it was considered daring when a woman picked up her skirts to cross the road. Men stared, just to catch a glimpse of her ankles so one can understand that tights were very, very, very . . . well, not quite nice!'

Hetty King dismissed this idea with a curt : 'Nothing of the kind.' Yet the appeal of the male impersonator is curious. To many people, the idea of a woman masquerading as a man is slightly 'off'. But why should Vesta Tilley's ambivalent cry of – 'Girls if you want to love a soldier, you can all love me !' be less sympathetic than a female impersonator inviting 'Come up and see me sometime.' Even delightful old newsreels of Hetty King entertaining troops in the First World War become uncomfortable when she starts slapping them on the back. The answer may lie in the instinctive attitude towards lesbianism and homosexuality. People tend to regard the former as . . . unnatural and unpleasant, and the latter as unnatural but entertaining. The threat of a woman usurping an active role, contrasted to the man adopting a passive one.

Ironically, though there is a strong element of homosexuality among female impersonators, this did not apply to the male impersonator. Don Ross said : 'Understandably they were always a target for lesbian approaches, yet having known them all I do not know of one who was in the least bit lesbian. In the time Ella Shields was with me, she begged me to go to the stage door many times to get rid of some girl or woman who persisted in calling and trying to insinuate herself.

'But I *have* noticed, both with Ella and Hetty King, that the moment they put on male attire their entire personality seemed to change, and remained changed until they were back in the dressing-room in a feminine gown.'

I asked Hetty King if she ever intended, like so many female impersonators, to resemble the part so perfectly that audiences might be confused. 'I don't think anyone ever thought that of Hetty King,' Hetty King replied. 'Perhaps some people wondered if she was masculine off-stage, one can't prevent what people think, but to me there is *nothing* more objectionable and I don't care who I offend, than a masculine woman.' (Ida Barr had spoken of an incident when Naomi Jacob came back-stage and as Hetty King refused to see her, Ida had welcomed her instead.)

'I loathe it. I find it horrible,' continued Hetty King. 'I'd always let them know there was a feminine there and after doing something tough, like spitting the tobacco juice out of my mouth, I'd look at the audience coyly.' She gave me a slight wink.

'I'd play a character which would remind them of a son or husband. What can one say? It was a nice performance. The only vulgarity is

now. Some of the things I see, well they make me a little bit . . . Sir
Oswald would never have allowed anything like that.'

As we talked, Hetty King grew less prickly and even seemed glad
to have company. She lived then in a tiny flat in a vast block near
Holborn, referring to it with distaste as her 'baggage room' and
indeed it was difficult to squeeze through the tiers of wardrobe trunks
stacked in the slim hallway. In the sitting-room there were no signed
photographs or playbills, no hint of the owner. She broke her rule of
two tots a day 'A tot at lunchtime and another after the show' –
and searched for glasses for a whisky and soda, muttering, 'I make a
good mistress but a lousy servant.' Her vitality was exceptional: 'I
don't go to parties,' was her brusque explanation.

Hetty King started when she was five years old, so that Marie's
début at the age of fifteen was comparatively late.

'Many times I was hidden under my step-mother's bustle when the
school board came to look for us, and I'd tickle her legs. Vaudeville
was tough. Glasgow one week, Dublin the next. But I was never
satisfied with two or three songs; it was always "Let me do it Daddy!"
Once I sang twenty-two songs at one go.'

'Did you wear boy's clothes off the stage?'

'Gosh no! None of that. Little socks and bonnets, father was very
strict.'

When she was ten, she was 'rented' out to people who acted as
managers. She told me of an incident in the dressing-room at the
'Metropolitan', where we made the record.

'I was crying because I'd been scolded and cuffed. The woman
who was with me ordered me to stop crying, and when I didn't she
hit me again. "Now stop that," she said. "If you don't you'll get
the biggest hiding of your life."

' "And what shall I be doing?" asked a fair-haired woman who
was making up at the other dressing place.

'The woman who was with me turned and stared – "You doing?
What? When?"

' "While you're giving the kid a hiding."

' "You'll mind your own business, that's what you'll do."

' "It'll be my business", said the fair woman, "to give you about
a hundred per cent more than you've ever given that kid in all your
life."

'Then she turned to me, very kindly. "Stop crying duck, and get yourself made up. No one's going to touch you while I'm here. No one."

'Later I sidled up to the fair woman and asked her name. "My name? Marie Lloyd. I'll look after you this week my pretty." '

Hetty King started to impersonate different acts the following year. 'Funnily enough they were always men, I never seemed to be interested in impersonating a woman. My chance came in 1903 at Bradford. I'm a great believer in fate and, as luck would have it, a manager was in front. He came round and said "My dear, you are going to be a great star one day." He offered me the part of Principal Boy but I said "I can't. I'm not tall enough."

'He offered me money that was a fortune in those days, £30 rising to £50 a week. I accepted and appeared at the 'Royal Court', Liverpool. I never looked back.

'Soon I reached three figures. I went to America and returned every two years. The money went up and up and I've been a head-liner ever since. To me a headliner is someone who's up there in lights fifty-two weeks a year, and you don't get that without your box-office.'

She explained the work that went into her act. 'That song about a man who goes to a party and gets terribly tight. People might think that easy, but it isn't. You must still behave like a gentleman, still try to walk as if one hadn't had a drop over the odds.

'When I did a navvy act I watched a man digging up the road opposite, for hours on end. He was a lazy bloke. He wouldn't bend down to pick up his shovel, he stepped on the end and caught it.

'For a sailor, I'd go down to the docks and board the freighters. I'd have to be careful, say "I just want to look over the boat" or they'd go shy. There was a sailor by the rail who'd take out his tobacco, cut it, roll it, and then light his pipe – all the time I'd be watching him.

'For a soldier, I was usually Scots Guards. My own tailor was military and every button was correct. I had my own hats and badges made especially small and the bayonet had to be miniature. My rifle was pukka, by permission from the War Office. I did the cheeky little Tommy going out for the evening. I studied one soldier who had a habit of twisting his cigarette with the side of his lip when he was talking – he wasn't very polite about it.

'For a padre, I'd go to church.

'The great Albert Chevalier came to see me at "The Coliseum". He said "Little lady, you are a *character* male impersonator. Never let up on that." '

Charles Chaplin was another admirer, but the favourite compliment came from a Sergeant Major who told his men : 'I've been drilling you lot for three months. Now go to "The Empire" and let a woman really show you how to do it.'

For underwear she had tight, black silk pants, and because her hair came down to her shoulders she disguised it with the help of a toupee.

Many of the famous songs of the First World War were written earlier, like *Tipperary* first performed in 1912, and she bought *All the nice girls love a sailor* in 1909 for £5. It almost failed at first for she played it as an officer – 'and officers didn't mean a sausage to the audience.' She burst into the *Ship Ahoy* chorus, with the gestures of lighting a pipe and throwing the match away, in perfect time.

'Did the song make you a lot of money?'

'It should have done.' She was reluctant to talk of her private life, and I had the feeling that none of her three marriages, one to the Music Hall singer Ernie Lotinga, had been particularly happy or lucrative

For sheer perseverance, Hetty King is a supreme example. She appeared in London at the old 'Mo', the 'Mogul Saloon' which became the 'Middlesex Music Hall', in 1897. She topped the bill at the 'Royal Hippodrome', Eastbourne in 1969. She still commands three figures. Incredibly, she is rather overlooked in the sentiment that now surrounds Music Hall. She never pampered her audiences or cajoled them for their love, she perfected the skill of her performance rather than its warmth.

Her integrity is touching. Artistically she is the last of her kind and like the end of a British Raj deserves a graceful, affectionate salute before the flag finally dips.

'Is the tradition of the male impersonator over?' I asked.

'Male impersonation means vaudeville. Where are the theatres? They're closed. Apart from myself, the male impersonators have gone.'

'Do you think this is a loss?' I should have known better.

'No,' she said simply.

'What has been your greatest triumph?'

'It's been triumph all the time,' she said emphatically. 'I've lived for my work and it has repaid me. A wonderful life.'

24 Wee Georgie Wood

Introducing the record MUSIC HALL, I said: 'The years of the great British Music Hall are almost over. Most of the theatres have been torn down. Many of the artists are no longer with us. But we have gathered together the artists who are carrying on the great tradition and are meeting for what is almost certainly the last time on this stage.'

As I write this now, fourteen years later, Hetty King is the only artist left of those who joined me at the 'Met' that afternoon. She is one of the two survivors of Music Hall who were real headliners in their time – the other is George Wood OBE.

Wee Georgie Wood is a poignant example of a star who was forced into show-business as a child and was never allowed to grow up. In a letter from him in March of 1971, he commented: 'From the time I brought £3 12 6 home to my mother from a concert she put me to work, and my own lost childhood is my reason for being opposed to child performers.'

There's probably no such thing as 'Child Impersonation', though Ivor Vintor before him and Jimmy Clitheroe afterwards, impersonated small boys when they were really middle-aged men. They were almost obliged to do this because of their height – or rather the lack of it. Little Tich escaped this fate, with his long, ski-like boots which he used as stilts, but he was so small that his name became part of the language.

He was named after the Tichbone claimant, a notorious music hall attraction, whose real name was Arthur Orton. He weighed twenty stone, and when Harry Ralph appeared on the same bill the manager is supposed to have said 'We have one very big "Tich" – now we'll have a little one.'

Georgie Wood was taken once to Tich's dressing-room: 'I laid my hand on his shoulder, "how nice to meet you," I said. He went into a frenzy.

' "Take the little bastard away," he screamed. 'Take it away!"
'Afterwards they told me: "Never touch him on the shoulder." '
'Tich showed his sensitivity. I had it but didn't show it so much.'

He told me also of his first meeting with Marie Lloyd. 'At twelve
and a half I'd burst into the Music Hall world as a headliner, rather
like the Beatles did later. I was one of the biggest box-office attractions, replacing "Consul" – the human chimpanzee. I still have the
gold watch I received in South Africa in 1909 for breaking all records.
In America I was billed as "The Boy Phenomenon".

'I met Marie in Glasgow where I was playing a nursery scene.
After Nanny had put me to bed, I dreamt of the Music Halls and
did imitations.'

Harry Lauder heard of this and demanded thirty shillings if he
continued to sing *Stop yer tickling Jock* – Or cut it out. But Marie
said: 'You're doing imitations aren't you ducks? You might as well
do it right dear.' He was impersonating Marie in her 'Directoire
dress' – but the dress was wrong, I leered instead of having a twinkle,
and my timing was slightly out. She coached me for three nights, had
me measured and bought me a real Directoire dress.

'I think she realized that I didn't get much joy in showing off. I
was missing an education and I wanted this more than anything else.
But I was made to be different. Marie sensed this.'

Marie saw the boy behind the performer. He was cruelly over-
worked. Starting at the age of five, he travelled from town to town
dodging the school inspectors, suffering the weekly ritual when
mothers took their stage children to be licensed by the magistrates.
'This dragging children into the courts with their sordid Monday
morning drunks and domestic cases is now, fortunately, a thing of the
past, but it was always a great worry to my child's mind. I had a
vague notion that if we did not get the permission it would be
through some fault of our own and that we should both be sent to
prison.'

In case there was any objection, his mother rehearsed him in a
little speech: 'I think it is a great pity that you will not permit me to
go on giving happiness...' but the licence was seldom refused. His
mother pushed him forward even when his voice was starting to fail –
'the vocal chords ruined by overmuch use'. He was nearing a breakdown when he was found by a policeman, wandering in London
alone and upset. He was eleven years old. After a short holiday he
was back at work again.

His act sounds sentimental today, but was popular then. In one of the 'Nursery at Bedtime' sketches, he played with a golliwog that came to life and danced. The golliwog was a lesser Music Hall artist called Arthur Stanley Jefferson who became world famous as 'Stan Laurel'.

Motherhood was a constant theme. In *Mama's Boy* he sang: 'And those that sneer will be the first to cheer. They'll be proud of Mama's Boy', and went off to war.

In a churchyard scene he played a little girl in a red wig as he sobbed on 'her' mother's grave: 'Oh Mother, if thou in heaven can hear thy Orphan child breathing her mournful prayer.'

Ida Barr appeared as his stage mother in a number of bills, but it was Dolly Harmer who became famous as his 'mother' over years, on stage and in films. When she died in 1956 he thought she was eighty, until he went through her papers and discovered her secret – she was ninety-four.

As for his real mother – 'Until I was ten I worshipped her, but then she was divorced from my father whom I adored.' He described how his father was so anxious 'for mother and me to be happy that he kept away.' One evening in 1940, Georgie Wood received an urgent phone call from a hospital saying there was a man who was asking for him, called Bamlett. That was Wood's real name. When he said he'd go there immediately they warned him it might be too late – and it was.

In his autobiography *I had to be Wee*, he speaks of his mother with 'pride and privilege . . . her never failing belief in me, her son.' But during our talk he unburdened himself of the lost childhood this 'belief' had cost him. 'It was more a case of my being weak than of her being strong. But she expected me to be like a trained dog. I was expected to have a great love for my mother.'

'And did you?' I asked.

'I think not,' he admitted, with difficulty. 'I had a conscience thing about her, upsetting myself that I ought to love her, pretending I did, and feeling guilty. I played on. It never occurred to her – she just accepted that I loved her and ought to give her everything. It would have been too brutal to disillusion her.'

'Was her ambition for you partly loneliness?'

'I think it was, you know. Though she on her part would never admit it, she was dissatisfied with my step-father.'

His mother died in 1946. Georgie Wood confessed, again with

difficulty, that he felt he was free : 'Now thank God I can really live.'

The year after his mother's death he made-up as 'the little boy' for the last time, at the 'Birmingham Hippodrome'. He continues to appear on stage and recited a recent curtain speech :

> I come before you with authority and diffidence.
> Authority, because I have mastered my craft.
> Diffidence, because unlike the bubble reputations
> Of those on the goggle-box, the Master realizes he is
> The Servant of the public.

He bowed and gave me a sharp glance : 'And that's *not* tongue in cheek.'

25 Music Hall revived?

In 1960 I moved into the East End. My new home was a small, old house above a barge-repair yard on the bend of the river at Limehouse, with a balcony over the water.

In the evening I explored the district and the local pubs. I discovered a wealth of entertainment on my own doorstep, pubs like music palaces with sovereigns of their own like Queenie Watts who belted out the blues at 'The Ironbridge Tavern', and Ray Martine who turned on his followers when they dared to heckle him at 'The Deuragon Arms'.

The range of talent was remarkable. 'The Eastern' at the corner of West India and East India Dock Road, where Conrad's Sea Captains stayed on shore, had an old-fashioned band with banjo and silver trumpet and a red-haired, one-eyed woman who sang, screamingly, *I 'ain't got nobody*. There was cool modern jazz at Bermondsey, just across the water; beat groups; and the usual female impersonators that the East End is so fond of. 'The Rising Sun' was the 'Palladium' of pub entertainment, with such regular stars as 'Welsh' George; Tex Withers, a hunchback with a horse who sang cowboy numbers, and a taxi-driver who impersonated Al Jolson.

Sunday lunchtime was especially lively, though faces were sallow from the night before. 'The Bridge House' at Canning Town was crammed with dockers and not a woman in sight apart from the girls who stripped on the stage. The dockers cheered as the clothes were discarded and then went home for Sunday lunch. I was dazzled. The pubs exploded with vitality and it seemed to me that Music Hall was back where it started.

Once again I planned a long-playing record and spent a number of evenings taping artists in pubs, including Ray Martine. The record company thought he was rather blue and lost interest in the whole idea. It was true the pub atmosphere did not come across on tape, so I thought of the obvious – television. It seemed ironic justice in the age of electronic entertainment which had helped to kill Music Hall, to make a programme on this revival in pubs where young audiences had the excitement of seeing *live* artists.

Ida Barr was brought out of retirement yet again and we filmed her in the ruins of 'Collins Music Hall' at Islington which had been spared the further humiliation of 'girlie' shows when it caught fire. Ida stood in front of the charred safety-curtain which proclaimed in large letters: 'What! Has this thing appeared again tonight? Hamlet.' We intended to fade this sequence into a pub, suggesting that Music Hall had gone full circle.

While I was making the television programme, which we called *Time Gentlemen Please*, I came across a derelict pub on the Isle of Dogs. 'The Newcastle Arms' was known locally as 'the pub with no beer' for it was often locked and always empty. One lunchtime, when the landlord had to go to another pub to fetch the drink I'd ordered, I asked him what was happening and he told me the pub was up for sale. The brewers wouldn't give him any more credit, which explained the absence of bottles, and he wanted to get out as soon as possible. It was 'on the floor' as they say, and no one wanted to take it over.

It was then, in a moment of madness, that I looked around me and thought it might be fun to run a pub.

It seemed the natural conclusion to my interests in the East End, the London river, pubs and Music Hall. I saw the brewers and within a month after an alarming appearance before the magistrates, I was the new landlord. For sentimental reasons I changed the name to 'The Waterman's Arms', for I discovered that my new home at Limehouse had been one of the many riverside pubs at the turn of the century, and this had been its name. Anyhow, 'The Newcastle Arms' seemed inappropriate.

I was lucky that the architect chosen by the brewers was Roderick Gradidge who not only understood my ideas but enhanced them with a brilliance of his own. He visualized the Music Hall saloon immediately. He knocked down a wall replacing it with a series of arches so that it was possible to look down on to the stage from the higher level of the public bar. An elaborate proscenium surrounding the stage was gilded with symbols of the Isle of Dogs and Music Hall names, such as Charles Morton, G. H. Elliot and, inevitably, Ida Barr.

The landlord at 'Collins' gave me one of the old gilt mirrors. Sam Collins, an Irish singer, had taken over the 'Landsdowne Arms' in 1863 and turned it into a Music Hall which kept his name though he died two years later when he was only thirty-nine. All that was left was the pub, still called 'The Landsdowne', and now this was demolished to make way for offices. I went to the auction and bid for a charcoal portrait of Harry Tate with his lop-sided moustache; a vast coloured poster of the comedian Tom Leamore dwarfed by a high wing collar; and old brown photos of Dan Leno, Little Tich and Marie Lloyd.

Don Ross gave me a splendid Bill of 'The London' in 1900 with the name of Marie Lloyd at the top, in great red letters. Ida Barr gave me various souvenirs and Marie Kendall signed one of her early song-sheets 'For Daniel, My Love, Marie Kendall, 1873–1963'.

I bought several hundred Victorian and Edwardian sheet music covers. The illustrations are a delight and provide an extraordinary mirror of an age. Every event, every scandal or battle, fashion, fad and foible was celebrated in song. Subjects ranged from Blondin crossing Niagara on a tightrope, to the Relief of Mafeking or Oscar Wilde on his lecture tour of America, posing beneath a giant sunflower.

At a time when the piano was the focal point of family entertainment, sheet music had an importance it lacks today and cost three or four shillings. The covers were magnificent examples of lithography.

The genius of the song-sheet artists was Alfred Concanen whose illustrations had a special wit and flamboyance. He sported a lengthy moustache himself, and parodied the fops and dandies with great affection, as in *Lord Dundreary's Galop*.

Most of the song-sheet artists – and there were only a few with real brilliance – drank to excess. It's hardly surprising for they worked for the most ephemeral of arts, destined as they must have thought for the dustbin and paper-mill. Even the lithographic stones were soon destroyed.

An early artist, Augustus Butler, was known as 'A Bohemian of Bohemians'. W. E. Imeson claims he had a weakness for 'what is known by ladies as white satin' – in other words gin. He drank so much that during a cholera epidemic he wandered about Soho quite happily while others fled from 'the street of the dead'. Doctors baffled by his immunity, concluded that he was so fortified with the spirit of his choice that he was rendered cholera proof.

Another great illustrator, Richard Childs, who portrayed General Gordon on the cover of *Too Late, Too Late* was also described as a man of irregular habits and died in hospital with a 'wrecked constitution'.

When he was a boy of sixteen, Gordon Craig saw Alfred Concanen drinking heavily in a tavern off the Strand. He died that night of apoplexy. Fortunately enough of his work has survived to show the care and detail he brought to his work, all the more touching when you realize how frustrated he must have been. Some covers were plainly commercial, but more than a hundred were designed with a love that still shines through.

These posters, photographs and covers were destined for the blood-red walls of 'The Waterman's'.

One morning I heard that the demolition men had moved into the 'Met'. I hired a van and raced to the Edgware Road where I paid the contractor thirty pounds to let me rescue what I could, after which he made life as difficult as possible. While 'The Met' fell, literally around me, three of us struggled with saws and axes and succeeded in saving a few cherubs, heads, caryatides and a box before the whole roof came crashing down. Souvenirs from the last theatre in London to operate as a genuine Music Hall. Several years later it was discovered that a mistake had been made in the council's calculations and the motorway was built several hundred yards to the side. The 'Met' was destroyed for nothing.

Finally I wrote to friends in show-business, asking them for signed photographs. I noticed it was the biggest and busiest star who responded most generously, like Tommy Steele, in the Music Hall tradition, who wrote : To my good pal Dan. Here's to a 'great gaff' and hoping I'm welcome any time. Your mate, Tommy.

The decorations were complete. After several dust-sheeted months, 'The Waterman's' was ready.

It seemed false modesty and very bad business not to include 'The Waterman's' in *Time Gentlemen Please!* which was almost completed. So the pub was shown in its new splendour, the brass and glass glittering as Ida Barr completed the song she had started in the ruins of 'Collins'. The programme also included a buxom girl called Kim Cordell, whom we filmed at 'The Rising Sun'. She attacked a song with such shattering personality that I knew we had found the resident singer and compere for our entertainment.

I liked *Time Gentlemen Please!*, but I was unprepared for the reaction. I watched it at 'The Waterman's' and when I returned to Limehouse, found I'd been burgled. The burglars must have broken into the house during the programme, assuming that I was doing it 'live' from the studio. The next morning I walked to the local paper shop, in case there were any reviews, and stopped in the street to look for them. They were raves. 'CHEERS FARSON' was the heading in the *Daily Mirror*, and underneath: 'Certainly this was streets ahead of the polished Hippodrome ... This is what Farson captured and presented, people enjoying themselves and entertaining without stilted formality – a cosiness that had both nostalgia and identity with the viewer sitting at home.' Dennis Potter, in a long article in the *Daily Herald* under the title 'LET US SEE *us* MORE OFTEN', said the programme: '... gave us an all too rare chance to balance the mid-Atlantic idioms of a wholly contrived pop-world with the rougher nuggets of a half-forgotten and older kind of tradition.'

Several newspapers referred to the theme of Music Hall. Claiming me as a Westcountryman, because my parents lived in Devon, the *Exeter Express and Echo* claimed I had – '... discovered what most people already knew – that the Music Hall as it has been known for generations has fled from the stage to the big London pubs. The result of this discovery is the programme *Time Gentlemen Please!* which has all the robustness and gaiety of the real Music Hall. I have for a long time been complaining that the Sunday night Palladium show is only a pale imitation and that I long for the real thing. On Wednesday night I found it –

'The singing had that richness and solidity that I suspect the old American jazz composers found in places like New Orleans – places from which they drew most of their inspiration.'

I quote these comments to show the extraordinary reaction.

For the next two days I was stopped constantly in the street by people who wanted to thank me for the entertainment. Usually only a few letters arrive, unless the programme is controversial, but this time I received several hundred asking for more.

The programme revealed an irony – that Music Hall was virtually over, but a hunger for it remained. Sulky Gower waving his stick as he sang *Here am I broken-hearted*, and Tommy 'Pudding' wearing his hat as he sang *Put a bit of treacle on your pudding Mary Anne,* came as a welcome relief after the pretty starlet.

The reaction was altogether so exciting, that I suggested a follow-up to the heads of the television company: travelling to Liverpool – this was just before The Beatles – and the working men's clubs of the North.

Instead, the company launched a synthetic pub show *Stars and*

Ida Barr at the Met on the last night, with the author and Miss Joan Littlewood.

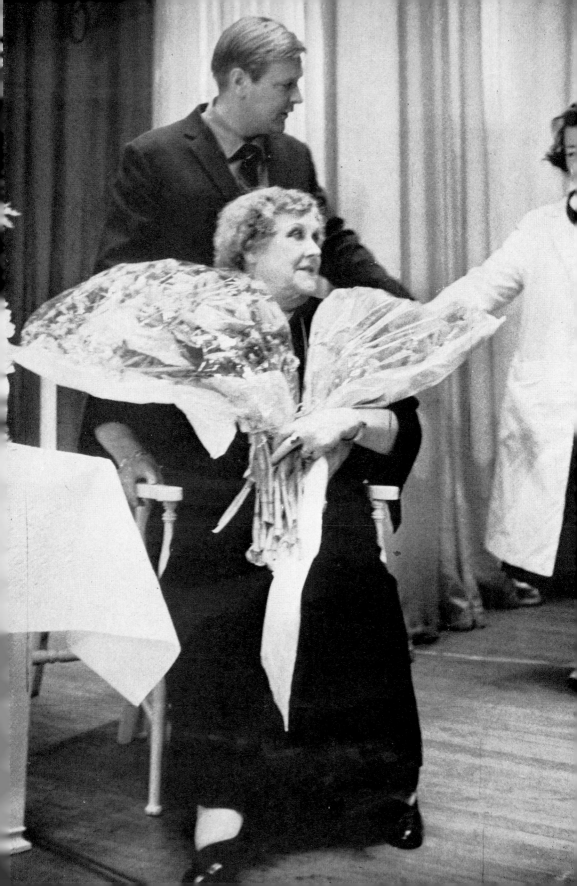

(Above) 'Nights At The Comedy': Mrs Shufflewick on stage.

(Left, opposite) Wee Georgie Wood. A portrait taken by the author.

Recording an L.P. at the Met. (Left to right): Music Hall veterans Hetty King, G. H. Elliott, Albert Whelan, Billy Danvers, Ida Barr and Marie Lloyd, Jnr.

ESPECIAL SA

"WHAT! HAS THIS THING
APPEARED AGAIN TO-NIGHT"
Hamlet.

SAFETY

Garters in a studio with extras drinking weak tea, staging fake punch-ups, and emotional moments with glycerine tears. It was the fake rather than the reality of real people performing in their own setting.

As for the original *Time Gentlemen Please!*, which was entered as the ITV choice in the Montreux Festival, the immediate result was a nightly invasion of the East End pubs by hordes of West Enders who dressed down for the occasion in sweaters and head-scarves and looked curiously out of place beside the immaculately turned-out locals. People pestered me for the addresses of the pubs in the programme and when I returned I was appalled to find that the whole atmosphere had changed. Writing in the *Sunday Times*, Maurice Wiggin remarked : 'In this new venture he is mining a rich vein of ore; if it doesn't give out he may well find himself setting a fashion.' All too prophetic.

Above all, the crowds flocked to 'The Waterman's Arms' which now had a reputation for Music Hall.

I doubt if any pub has ever been visited by such an *unlikely* assortment of celebrities. Tony Bennett, Groucho Marx and Claudette Colbert, Lord Boothby and Lord Montagu, Frankie Howerd and Trevor Howard, Jacques Tati who was brought by Joan Littlewood, Bernard Delfont, David Merrick, Brian Epstein, Norman Hartnell, Cyril Lord, and Mary Quant, Joe Brown, Sybil Burton and Ken Tynan, Godfrey Winn, Billy Walker ... the list is endless. The Visitors' Book had one page with the signatures of Lady Diana Cooper, and Lady Aberconway; another had Francis Bacon and Bill Burroughs, the author of *The Naked Lunch*, and Emlyn Williams.

At the end of one evening, the crowded pub fell silent as Shirley Bassey sang *I Who have Nothing* – when she was unmistakably pregnant; another time I gave a party for Judy Garland. News of this got round beforehand and her star appeal was greater than I realized. When she arrived, an hour or so late, the pub was so full and she looked so frail that we had to form a battering ram to make a path for her. It happened to be the hottest night of the year and when the crowds and noise and heat became so intense that she almost fainted, I took her upstairs to the large private room I used for

Ida Barr being filmed for 'Time Gentlemen Please!', in the ruins of Collins Music Hall, Islington.
The end of the Met. As demolition men worked around him, the author tried to save some of the plaster decoration.

parties, and she sat on the balcony in the slight breeze that came from the river.

After closing time she decided she wanted to sing. My manager said it was against the law to turn on the lights again in the saloon.

'To hell with that,' said Judy Garland, 'I'll pay the fines.' But the manager was adamant and she sang by the moonlight that came through the large glass windows. Someone started to play the opening notes of *Come rain or come shine*. She listened closely, and with a sudden snap of the fingers spun round and started to sing for the few of us .

That was a moment of magic. So were the evenings around Christmas and New Year's, when we had the extra hour which was always needed so badly. I remember the first Christmas, before too many tourists made it impossible to move, when the old pub was filled with East Enders singing the old songs like *Knees Up Mother Brown* without a trace of affectation, literally dancing for joy. Then the whole thing seemed worthwhile.

For if my descriptions of the apparent success of 'The Waterman's' smack of conceit – it is a very small conceit. I had achieved the impossible – 'The Waterman's' was too successful, so crowded that it was literally a struggle to get a drink, and our entertainment so popular that people preferred to listen, and do their hard drinking elsewhere. But that is another story. Outwardly it seemed a triumph; 'The Waterman's' was photographed and filmed and listed as part of so-called 'Swinging London'.

As for Music Hall, there were certain evenings when at least a flavour of Variety was captured, through sheer pace and contrast. Kim Cordell, eyelids flashing with green and gold sequins, roared out the old favourites. Friends like jazz singers George Melly and Annie Ross were never too grand and always ready to get up on the stage. Ida Barr might be followed by a Beat Group, Karl King (who was only fourteen years old) and the Vendettas. A man banged his head with a tin tray to the tune of *Mule Train*, and a girl who was known as 'The White Mouse' sang so off-key that she was greeted with cheers whenever she appeared and became a favourite.

The question remained: was the Music Hall atmosphere that I was striving for just a matter of a passing night or two, or could it be taken further? Colin Macinnes suggested at the time that I become an impressario. He wrote in *New Society*: 'Most of us have fantasies we fail to bend into realities, but Mr Dan Farson has – to coin a phrase – made his dream come true. And not content with realizing his own dream, Mr Farson has realized one of mine : which is that popular song and entertainment should evade the telly screens and radio to which they have been banished from the few surviving Theatres of Variety and reappear, as they did in their days of authenticity and glory, on a performer-to-audience basis where there is direct, personal communication.'

26 Nights at the Comedy

An opportunity arose for a Pub-type show in the West End. This was being presented by William Donaldson, a young producer who backed *Beyond the Fringe* when others had lost faith. I went to see him and he asked me to devise the show. A few days later, I found myself with Donaldson in the office of Bernard Delfont. Delfont is one of those rare people who can make a decision in a moment. At the time I was unaware of his power and took him at his face value as a person who knew what he was talking about and expressed a genuine affection for Music Hall which dated from the time when he had been a dancer on the Halls himself. He asked what I had in mind.

I explained my concept of a boisterous type of new Music Hall, rather than a reconstruction with a chairman and hammer. I mentioned various artists and Delfont stopped me sharply when I came to *Mrs Shufflewick*: 'No, he's wrong. He sends Music Hall up.'

Now the one artist I was absolutely certain of was Mrs Shufflewick, or rather Rex Jamieson. I had seen him in the bill on the last night of 'The Met' and spoke to him in the bar afterwards, asking him to appear at 'The Waterman's' which he had done regularly with great success.

'Broad-minded to the point of obscenity', Tipsy-genteel in a flowered hat, Mrs Shufflewick begins by fingering a dreadful piece of fur – 'You like this . . . it was given me by a hundred men who gave me a pound each, so I wasn't done was I? I can't remember myself the gin and tonic has fogged the brain – I'm happy to say'. And went on to recount the drunken disasters of the night before, which ended when she found herself sitting stark naked on top of a 29 bus.

'I don't think that's fair,' I protested. 'To my mind Mrs Shufflewick *is* Music Hall.' Donaldson flinched, but Delfont leant forward and pressed a switch on his intercom which connected him to his adviser Billy Marsh.

'What does the name Mrs Shufflewick mean to you?' he asked. There was a pause, 'If it's anything to do with Music Hall there's no one better, but . . .' 'Thanks,' said Delfont, and turned to me:

'All right then, go on.'

I left Donaldson to cope with the business arrangements, but in due course, for his own excellent reasons, Delfont withdrew.

The show took shape but the discipline of the Delfont organization would have proved invaluable. I had spoken to Jimmy Tarbuck in Leeds and he agreed to appear in the show, but not as the compère. This was our main problem. Donaldson came up with an interesting choice – Nicol Williamson who was then unknown to the general public.

I remember the first meeting of the cast at a room in the YMCA which smelt of wet carpet, on a depressing morning in December. The cast had little in common and took an instinctive dislike to each other. Sulky Gowers arrived dressed like an old-time gangster, very smart; the Red Indians looked cold and moth-eaten; Tarbuck suspicious but successful; and Nicol Williamson, in a worn leather jacket and docker's boots, hunched his shoulders in such depression that Tarbuck asked me what on earth he was doing there.

Williamson was the next to withdraw. This time I had an idea. On a visit to Manchester I had been impressed by the 'New Luxor Club', which resembled a converted aircraft-hangar and achieved the right, raffish atmosphere in a breathless succession of turns ranging from high-wire acrobats to grand opera. The clubland of the North was staging its own revival of Music Hall, as valid as that in the East End pubs.

Throughout the evening at the 'Luxor', a compère loped about the stage. Part of his charm lay in his appearance – it was so wrong: a large middle-aged man with spectacles who looked as if he should have been some place else. His name was Jacky Carlton and I persuaded Donaldson to hear him. Carlton arrived on the day of final auditions, slightly sweating. In the prettiness of the Comedy Theatre he looked more out of place than ever. On stage, a popular young comedian from a television panel game was going through his act which was bright and efficient. Donaldson was thankful to settle for him but I hurried down and took him aside: 'This poor man,' I waved towards the bulky figure in the stalls, 'has come all the way from Manchester thinking this is his big chance. Do at least hear him.'

'Very well,' said Donaldson. 'Tell him we've got the compère, but we might be able to give him a "spot".' I didn't have the heart to tell Carlton this when I rejoined him. Instead I said : 'This is it. If you go out there and work as you've never worked before, there might still be a chance. Imagine it's the first night, and the theatre is full.'

Carlton filled 'The Comedy' with his imaginary audience, heckling and greeting the people he recognized. 'God he's brilliant,' whispered Donaldson. 'If he's only half as good as this on the first night, our troubles are over.' He went on stage and told a perspiring Carlton that he was the compère. The television comedian offered his congratulations with the generous comment – 'After what I've just seen, I don't blame you.'

On 8 January (1964) *The Times*: 'Music Hall Returns to the West End', and the *Telegraph*: 'Music Hall at Four London Theatres', both ran a news item released by the Music Hall Society which referred to a 'tremendous revival of Music Hall' and revealed we had rivals. I wanted to call our show 'New Music Hall', but after one of the rivals was withdrawn, called 'Nights at the Tivoli', and another rival was announced as 'Fielding's Music Hall', Donaldson chose 'Nights at the Comedy'. Not realizing that competition could only be good for us, we raced ahead in order to be first.

I was in that state of euphoria which hits people before the opening and blinds them to all reality. I lived in a daze of first-night telegrams and box-office returns, blissfully ignoring the warning signals in front of me. There were too many people making decisions for one thing; myself, Donaldson, his new backer Michael Winner, and the ever-patient director Eleanor Fazan. There were far too many people in the show itself. We booked enough turns to ring the changes every fortnight, but in trying to consolidate the first night we swamped it. More and more people joined the cast. We discussed possible readings from Dickens with Finlay Currie and auditioned Katina the astrologer. We excluded them for some reason, yet included a boxer called The Islington Tiger, who challenged members of the audience, and introduced a beer drinking contest of a yard of ale.

Suddenly the First Night had begun, and the full terror of it replaced the euphoria as I sat in the back of a box. The curtain rose and Kim Cordell came on simply and sang *If you were the only boy in the world* straight and strong. The impact was great. Mrs Shufflewick followed and we were away.

Jimmy Tarbuck made his first appearance in the West End, and

Jimmy James his last. I had been too worried during the rehearsals
to notice that his mind was wandering and his two stooges had to
improvise swiftly as he changed his lines. Now I saw that the act was
so irrelevant it hardly mattered. His two stooges were masters of
dead-pan self-effacement. One was red-nosed with an ankle-length
overcoat who came in with the line : 'Here! Have you been putting
it about that I'm barmy?' The audience plainly loved the jokes all the
more because of their familiarity.

One of the stooges, holding a cardboard-box, announced that he
had two lions.

'Are they in that shoe-box?' asked Jimmy James casually.

'Yes.'

'I *thought* I heard a rustling.'

During the interval, there was a buzz of enjoyment.

Afterwards, there was the first set-back when one performer was
so off-form I couldn't imagine what was wrong. Then I realized, and
lay on the floor of the box groaning. Several of the cast were heavy
drinkers and elaborate precautions had been taken to protect them.
No one expected trouble from this artist whose performance was
described by *The Times* the next morning as 'acutely embarrassing'.

Ida Barr revived the atmosphere with an entrance worthy of a
star, dressed in her usual black velvet, with her silver-topped cane,
dangling lorgnette and chiffon handkerchief. She waved away the
microphone with a gesture of contempt that was welcomed with
cheers : 'take this *thing* off.'

The show should have ended there, but though it cried out for
cutting we had kept a space at the end for 'Astonishing Guest
Artist'. Donaldson had chosen The Alberts, who died the 'death of a
dog' as Hetty King might have said. The whole tension collapsed and
it was all the more bitter to know that Joe Brown had offered to
appear out of friendship to close the evening with Music Hall songs
like *Knocked 'em in the Old Kent Road*.

In the grip of first night deception, I forgave The Alberts and
toured the dressing-rooms with a special visit to Ida Barr who was
surrounded by flowers and visitors in a state of genuine surprise. At
a party afterwards, a woman who was not connected with the show,
told me : 'You really *are* on top of the world, aren't you?', stunned
that anyone could be so naïve.

Yet the papers were kind. 'Music Hall has come back to the West
End' said the *Express*, and the *Daily Mirror* after calling it 'An

evening of nostalgia, cheerful vulgarity, raucous singing ... a wild, wild evening', said it was a brave attempt to bring the old Music Hall back and could well succeed. The critic concluded – 'The only clean crack all evening was made by an Indian with a whip.'

Mrs Shufflewick was the outstanding success and it was right that many people were genuinely shocked. In a parody of himself, Harold Hobson was lyrical in the *Sunday Times* though he described pubs as 'repellent institutions' : '... in strange justification of it all, there is Mrs Shufflewick, a refined lady with a skimpy fur and a red nose – Mrs Shufflewick times her amazing lines more accurately than Mussolini did his trains. I call them amazing, because that is what they are. In words that might be used by earnest workers at a Mothers' Union meeting, Mrs Shufflewick advances propositions and recounts adventures that would make Rabelais blush. Mrs Shufflewick glides around equivocal corners with a genteel but genuine verbal grace. She conveys things which were, and still are, denied to Frank Harris. Yet there is no offence i' the world. No objectionable word passes those quietly challenging lips – well, only one and even to *that* I don't suppose anyone but me would object. She is overwhelmingly and shatteringly funny. She manifests that heart-warming, honest vulgarity we hear so much about, and which in practice usually is nothing but cant. She is also very relevant to the serious theatre.

'... when it comes to ingenuity and wit, this Mrs Shufflewick, innocently appalled at the things that happen to her, leaves them standing.

'... she inspires the hope that freedom of thought and restraint of language will endure among clever people for a long time yet.'

Mrs Shufflewick appeared early on the bill, so we spent much of the evening drinking together in the 'Comedy' bar. I noticed that as Rex Jamieson he was quiet and unassuming, but dressed as Mrs Shufflewick, as he was then, he revealed a forceful personality. Almost as if the role had devoured his own identity.

Jacky Carlton never did recapture the first brilliance of that audition, largely because so many people were giving him conflicting directions, and returned thankfully to Manchester. He was replaced by William Rushton. But the show settled down though it was still untidy and by the third week the charabanc trade were making their reservations. On the fourth Saturday we had a full house for the first time. Half an hour before the curtain went up, so did a notice from Donaldson stating this was the last performance – a notice to close.

The failure of the show was trivial to the financial failure of 'The Waterman's', as far as I was personally concerned.

I realized too late that I had placed myself in a lunatic position, at the mercy of everyone, quite apart from myself. There was the basic flaw that we didn't have time to sell enough drink to cover the cost of our entertainment. Closing time at eleven and the inability to charge an entrance fee, made it impossible. The profit on a barrel of beer is negligible. When a manager proved incompetent, I couldn't sack him on the spot but had to find someone acceptable to the magistrates and go through all the rigmarole of the courts in replacing his name as the other licensee.

The solution was to leave 'The Waterman's' immediately, but this proved difficult. I was under notice to the brewers who kept me waiting until they fond a new tenant who would accept their terms for 'going in'. This payment was for the goodwill built up over the last few years which would have come to me if it had been a 'free house'. So I was placed in the nightmare position of pouring money into 'The Waterman's' month after month to cover the losses. It all seems inconceivable now and all the more bitter because 'The Waterman's' was such a spectacular success in every other way.

Soon after the closure of *Nights at the Comedy* I resigned from my job in television. I was stale from life in London; I wanted to get back to the sea – to my house on the coast of North Devon. There I wrote a television play for the BBC called *The Frighteners*. The story editor was Harry Moore and afterwards he sent me a letter: 'A sudden thought! Is there a Music Hall character – dead? Whose life might make a musical? Does such an idea attract you?' He moved down to Devon with his wife and family and we worked on the story of Marie Lloyd under the title of *Thanks for Nothing* for three rain-drenched weeks until his children fell ill and had to be taken back to London. As I continued on my own, with growing excitement, I wondered why nobody had thought of the subject before. I discovered they had. Herbert Wilcox had planned a film with Anna Neagle; Pat Kirkwood played Marie in an early BBC television programme in 1955, which didn't even mention the arrest on Ellis Island; Dora Bryan told me she had been asked to play her in a stage production; and Hattie Jacques, Hermione Baddeley and Beryl Reid had all been interested at various times in portraying her too.

MARIE LLOYD and Music Hall

There were even rival musicals waiting to go into production. Cecil Madden wrote to me that he had been working on one for years called *Don't Dilly Dally* and we heard that Ned Sherrin was collaborating with Caryl Brams on a 'book' for H. M. Tennent. Trying to forestall them, we announced ours in *The Times* (20 December 1966): 'A recently completed musical on the life of Marie Lloyd is due for a large-scale London production next year.' This prompted Sherrin to announce his musical, with music by Ron Grainer.

The composer of our new music was Norman Kay, whose ebullience proved very necessary; I wrote the lyrics. Ted Kotcheff agreed to direct and started to shape our 'book' with swift professionalism. Suddenly he had to leave for America, but it was arranged that tapes of the new music should be sent to Bernard Delfont who was 'interested'. This was our first mistake. Racing ahead foolishly, in order to get in first, we fixed a studio session and to save further time Norman used singers who could read music straight off. They did this with technical skill but no meaning whatsoever. The result sounded like a dreadful operetta, though we were too bemused to realize it at the time. The tapes were sent to Delfont, who rejected the idea, and Ted Kotcheff groaned aloud when he heard them on his return.

We then sent the script to Joan Littlewood whom I had worked with previously. She had always loved the subject and told me once that she wanted Barbara Windsor to play it.

There was no reaction, a long silence, and then on a glorious summer's day in Devon I was called from the garden and there was Joan on the phone saying all the things that any author longs to hear. Elated I came to London to see her at 'The Theatre Royal', Stratford East where she first produced *A Taste of Honey*; *The Hostage*; and *Oh, What a Lovely War*.

Over the road hung bedraggled bunting reading MUSIC HALL, only some of the letters had fallen off so it didn't mean anything at all. Gradually I realized that the entertainment she was presenting with her 'nuts' was upstairs in the pub opposite and a hat went round afterwards. The 'Theatre Royal' was leased temporarily to someone else. It was rather a shock.

We discussed casting and agreed that Marie should be played by Avis Bunnage, but the meeting left me in a state of suspense. It was all so vague. There was no definite assurance that Joan Littlewood was going to produce it at all. However, she did tell me that Sherrin and Brahms had shown her their script several years earlier and she had turned it down.

I suspected that her final approval depended on the reaction of Avis Bunnage, and she proved enthusiastic. We arranged another recording session, this time with Avis alone and Norman at the piano instead of the twitter of sight-readers. This time the result was powerful especially in Marie's original songs which Avis performed with none of that archness which so many imitators adopt today and which is ultimately so patronizing. When Joan and Gerry Raffles heard this new tape they were astonished and phoned her the moment it was over: 'Avis you've never been better. It's thrilling. You're marvellous.'

After numerous delays and doubts, Joan decided to go ahead with the production. I descended on Stratford East, all too often as it turned out, where the atmosphere was now buoyant with the success of *Mrs Wilson's Diary* which was being transferred to the West End. Joan was on top again.

Angel Lane, which led to the theatre, resembled a Littlewood stage-set of cockney-land, lined with colourful stalls and pie-shops, with long black eels slithering in shallow boxes, cockles and winkles, and ribald greetings from stall-holders all the way. The lunchtime 'caff' was managed by two old women who screamed endless messages – 'Joanee. One of yer young fellers been in for yer – Joan.' I had been looking forward to interesting little talks with her, but was lucky to get a word in over the ham and chips and powerful cups of tea. I began to hate the good humour of the place.

But back in the theatre we got down to details of casting, sets and costumes. Joan decided on the more direct title – *The Marie Lloyd Story*. The contracts arrived and so did an argument of agents. We heard privately that Sherrin's musical had been dropped.

Of course I knew of Joan Littlewood's formidable reputation, that many actors are made by her and some destroyed, but that no one who works with her is ever quite the same again. I had seen the vitality of her productions, but knew also that they could become battlegrounds, that the first night of *Twang* in Manchester had been an epic disaster with actors receiving their lines as they went on stage and the audience rising in anger. I knew of Ken Tynan's remark, made in admiration, that if she'd lived several hundred years earlier she'd have been burnt as a witch. I knew that she was a law to herself alone and that like Marie Lloyd every conflicting thing they said about her might be true. I knew she had the most disarming smile of any woman I had met, though the signature at the bottom of her notes was worrying – J. Hell'.

But every suggestion she made was right and strengthened the 'book'. On the Sunday before the first week of rehearsal, I had dinner in her large house at Blackheath and she explained everything she was doing and why. I returned to Limehouse soon after midnight, relieved and happy.

The next afternoon I ambled into the theatre to find it full of people doing extraordinary things, like a grown woman being dragged across the stage howling like a baby.

I thought *Mrs Wilson's Diary* must be odd. Then it dawned on me, this was *Marie*. Not a word of our dialogue remained; I failed to realize this is how Joan works, to begin with. Stricken, I fell out of the theatre and phoned Harry Moore who was in the middle of filming a horror programme for television and sounded suicidal.

The next morning Joan was busy with the transfer of *Mrs Wilson's Diary*. Bob Grant, her assistant, was saying: 'Let's play the party scene again, as if it was ballet.'

'That's strange,' I thought. 'It sounded as if he said ballet.' Ballet he said and ballet he meant.

Thinking if I can't fight them I might as well join them, I played an old man in a queue in one of the 'games'. Harry arrived and sat in the stalls looking white and aghast. Joan looked in and noticed him. Later I had tea with some of the actors in the caff and *thought* I got on rather well with them. Indeed, by the next morning the first shock was beginning to fade, especially when Joan took the trouble to explain certain points to Norman Kay and myself. She had asked us to write a song for a character loosely based on Fred Barnes, the matinée idol who was ruined after a scandal involving a sailor in Hyde Park. Instead of making this character a female impersonator, Joan and I thought it would be more fun to have him dressed immaculately in a white suit singing tough cowboy numbers which 'got the bird'. I wrote lyrics for the song which was meant to be terrible but proved one of the most popular in the new score. It was called *The Great Outback* –

> I'm on my way to the great outback
> And the wide open spaces

Where the sun glares down and cracks the ground
And the men have dusty faces.

I had phoned these, and equally awful words to Norman who had
written a rollicking tune. Now, as we sat in the stalls, he gave a sudden
bellow as he read the lyrics and came to the end of the first verse –
'And yearn for a girl's embraces' – On the phone it sounded like 'And
yearn for a girl in braces.' We sobbed with idiotic laughter, partly
relief that everything seemed to be going well after the initial shock.
Joan Littlewood stopped for a second on stage and stared.

Joan was rehearsing the opening scene, a band-call at Sheffield on
a Monday morning, and told us how miraculous this had been the
day before : 'I wish you'd been here.' Now the cast improvised again,
but with less success and when Joan asked Norman what he thought
of the scene he was tactful and enthusiastic, but he suggested it
could be tightened up a bit.

Studying her notes, hurrying from one actor to another, I realized
a few minutes later that she was talking to me :

'It's no good. I can't go through with it. It's not going to work.' I
gave a ghastly smile.

'I'm miserable,' she continued, 'you're miserable.'

'But Joan,' my throat had gone dry. 'I couldn't be happier. I agree
with everything you've suggested.'

'I can't work this way. I'm an egomaniac, no I'm not, it's just that
I'm too old. I don't care if I break people's hearts. This is the only
way I can work. I did this with Brendan and Shelagh and my other
nuts and it worked.' She referred to her 'Private Eye nuts' and how
she had changed every word they had written, with success. Also to
Wolf Mankowitz who had expected her to stick to his script, 'but I
can't work like that.'

She said all this softly, looking at me over her half-spectacles, with
their thin metal frames.

'I don't think you know a thing about the theatre. I don't believe
you can write dialogue. Norman comes here and has the audacity to
tell me what to do, Harry sits there looking like death and upsets the
actors. I can only work my way. I thought you understood that.'

I stood there mesmerized. The words came like bullets yet to anyone watching we might have been having a friendly talk. Norman sat
beaming in the stalls. For a moment Joan was called away, but she

came back to add, as if to make sure that the corpse was dead, 'And you, you're too concerned.'

'Wouldn't it be awful if I wasn't?' I managed to say.

'I mean it. I'm dead serious.' She gave me a cold look and walked away.

The rehearsals continued, without us.

Of course she was right. I was too concerned. We had worked on the script for too long and too hard. We had supplied her with a finished article when she would have been happier with a few pages of outline to build on. As for the new music, Norman Kay was the first to agree later that the old Music Hall numbers were so remarkable they could hardly be improved on or added to in this unique context.

At the first rehearsal of *The Frighteners*, I had told the director that I wouldn't mind if the cast wanted to change their words. He snapped back: 'No actor in any production of mine alters a single word of the script.' Now I experienced the other extreme; unfortunately the actors at Stratford, who made up their own words as they went along, wrote even worse dialogue than I did.

Even so, in spite of all the dramas and traumas off-stage, it came tantalizingly close to success on stage. With a few simple strokes, Joan was able to achieve effects that were more spectacular than those of any Drury Lane production with revolving stages. There were moments of magic, that only she could produce.

There were two first nights. On the first I arrived as the lights began to dim. They were a tough audience. Certain knock-about scenes plainly bored them, but they were intrigued. Avis Bunnage was absolutely true and slowly won them over. At the end of the first half when she sang *My Old Man*, some members of the audience started to sing with her, quite spontaneously, very softly at first, until suddenly I realized that the whole theatre was joining in. This, for me, was the best moment of the whole production.

The critics were fair. Milton Shulman wrote: 'the book seems to have been mauled in the production' and *The Times* made a surprising comment on the *lack* of 'the usual reports of disagreement between Joan Littlewood and her writers' but added – 'the story-line is consistently sabotaged by the impulse to keep things lively'.

Frank Marcus actually voted for it as the best musical of the year, and in spite of the cold and the pre-Christmas preoccupation, the 'Theatre Royal' seemed to glow with success. The show improved nightly and the one person Joan never spared was herself. The transfer was never in doubt, with agents bargaining over percentages of the riches to come. And time ran out. The West End Manager who provided half of the backing, while I raised the other, decided against a transfer at the last moment. The box-office was doing excellent business but it was too late : the lease of the 'Theatre Royal' had been sold to another company which took over on Boxing Day.

I phoned Joan and Gerry suggesting a farewell drink and we met half-way between Stratford and the West End in a crowded Aldgate pub teeming with colourful cockney characters that might have been figments of her imagination.

This is my last memory of Joan Littlewood. Not the tough taskmaster with the shadow-boxing gestures and those sinister half-specs, now she looked like a young girl.

Touched and flattered by an incident that morning, she showed me the mink cap that the local children – her 'nutters' – had given her after she'd spoken up for them in the magistrates court.

'Nicked it, I suppose,' she said proudly.

The Littlewood production was never revived. A new version written by myself with the old songs only was presented by the 'Theatre Royal', Lincoln, in May 1969. Directed with discipline by Philip Hedley and played with flair the first night was sufficiently successful for Ray Cooney Productions to commission it for the West End. After several months of re-writing, the book was ready for a try-out at the 'Theatre Royal', Windsor. With the experience gained from his own successful farces, Ray Cooney wished to have everything right before the show was launched in a large-scale production in the West End, and possibly on Broadway.

Suddenly Ned Sherrin's version was revived and presented at Greenwich, with Barbara Windsor as Marie Lloyd. Rightly or wrongly, it's considered commercial suicide to have two musicals on the same subject and our 'Marie' was doomed the moment that Sing a Rude Song came into the West End. It made no difference that it ran for only a few weeks.

The story of Marie Lloyd is still a fine subject for a musical. Meanwhile, I have to face the unpleasant knowledge that this has been a catalogue of failure.

27 The Fall of the Curtain

The end of the Stratford production was the end of my association with Music Hall.

It closed on Christmas Eve 1967. Marie Lloyd Junior, who had tried to stop the production at one point, died on the Boxing Day. Poor Marie Junior: it can't have been much fun to spend a lifetime impersonating a mother she never really liked. Conversely, in spite of the early devotion and their tours together, it seemed as if Marie never understood her daughter.

A story has it, that once they were on the same bill together and Marie heard her daughter's act through the loudspeaker in her dressing-room.

'That one,' she said to a companion, 'will never make a star as long as she's got a hole in her arse.'

When I took Marie Junior (whose real name was Mrs Aylin) to 'The Ivy' for lunch and asked about the past, she was curiously uninterested whenever her mother was mentioned. Apart from a few, familiar anecdotes she had little to say.

Yet if she hadn't been consumed by her mother's fame, she might have been a performer in her own right. She gives a lively rendering of *Cromwell* on the MUSIC HALL LP, and sang *The Girl Who'd Never Had Her Ticket Punched Before* with considerable spirit one evening at 'The Waterman's'. But they were her mother's songs.

Her death was unreported in the press.

Ida Barr had died earlier on 17 December. Totally distracted by the show, I hadn't seen her for several weeks when I heard she was dying and had been asking for me. I went to the hospital, as grim as a dungeon, and found her in a long public ward, overcrowded, or so it seemed, with a hundred other old people. Her face was devoid of colour, there was no familiar smile or attempt to rally – 'Oh, why won't they let me go?' she asked, and that was really all she wanted. She refused to eat, she had given up, and the next time she didn't recognize me. I wished she could have died suddenly in the gaiety of her own room.

Apart from this ending, the friendship with Ida Barr had been one of the better aspects of my love affair with Music Hall.

After I had shown her on television for the first time, Danny La Rue spoke to me at a party about her splendid appearance, 'I'm so glad she's one of the few who were able to save some money.' I explained that she lived in a tenement on public assistance and her old-age pension which came to £3 13s a week. Under some callous regulation, any fee she now received was deducted. Danny La Rue, then comparatively unknown, looked disconcerted.

Several days later he phoned to say he had arranged a surprise Benefit and would I bring her to a club in Brixton. When we arrived Ida was greeted by a crowd of film stars and aristocratic villains; Danny La Rue and his friends gave a complete Music Hall Show. As this was meant as a surprise I hadn't told her about the Benefit and this was a mistake – she was mystified, and confused, too overwhelmed to sing one of her old numbers in spite of cries of encouragement. When the owner of the club presented her with a cheque, she stuffed it straight into the caverns of her handbag which put a slight damper on the climax of the evening. Later, I saw her take the cheque out surreptitiously and she burst into tears when she realized the Benefit had given her eight hundred pounds. It was characteristic of Danny La Rue that he kept in the background and received less recognition than anyone, though this was entirely his own idea and must have cost him a lot in time and trouble.

For Ida £800 was a fortune. It enabled her to buy the luxuries that can make such a difference to life – at any age.

It's satisfying also to remember that she became a star again when all such hopes were over. Because of television, it's probable that she was seen by more people in those last few years than by Marie Lloyd in all her lifetime. New friends, a new fame brought a bonus to the end of her life, like an unexpected treat.

When the 'Met' did finally close, Ida was the main attraction on the last night. Afterwards I introduced her to Joan Littlewood as she sat on the stage vast and resplendent in her old black velvet surrounded with bouquets and fifty red roses sent by the stall-holders of Berwick Market where she did her shopping.

'Ida,' said Joan Littlewood, 'I think you are the richest woman I have ever met.'

'I've known such lovely people in my life,' Ida told me later, 'I don't know what I've done to deserve it, that so many people should be so good to me.' The answer lay within herself.

My association with 'The Waterman's Arms' is over but a commemorative 'Ida's Bar' was opened there as part of an extension on 16 November 1971. The front is part of the box I rescued from the ruins of the old 'Met', and the back is decorated with souvenirs that Ida left me in her Will.

28 A People's Entertainment

In 1930 Oswald Stoll declared : 'Conventional Variety is dead'. He should have known, for his personal censorship helped to kill it along with radio, the 'talkies', and the death blow from television yet to come.

But forms of variety continue and will always do so as long as there's entertainment. The 'Palace Theatre', where they held the Royal Command Performance in 1912, recently presented a bill with Danny La Rue and Roy Hudd that was in the old tradition.

Stoll meant that Music Hall was dead. This was becoming true. Music Hall belonged to its time and that time was nearly over. Everything changed after the First World War.

As early as 1933, only three years after the obituary by Stoll, the 'Garrick Theatre' staged 'Old Time Music Hall'. Already it was a thing of the past. Today, 'Old Tyme Music Hall' is a popular feature of the seaside Summer Show. Indeed Music Hall has acquired such a venerable glow that it's hard to remember it was once despised as the lowest form of entertainment and not for the family at all.

I have made, and stretched the point that Music Hall has returned to the music pub. It is true they have much in common, both are a people's entertainment, and that is surprisingly rare.

In the pub you can still find the original performer rather than the copy. The compère is known to many of the regulars; there is no attentive hush; if people are bored they drown the act with noise – if they are entertained they join in spontaneously with none of the condescension of song-sheets. However young, the customers know the old songs which have proved indestructible.

The pub entertainer has to rise above the chatter and the clatter of crates by sheer force of personality, just as the Music Hall artist had to command attention without the help of a microphone. Both are solitary performers, and vulnerable. The pub entertainer has absolute contact with his audience, but he is out on his own with no support; the Music Hall artist seldom met the others on the same bill.

Above all, the atmosphere of a music pub or a working men's club is like that of the old hall – tough and gloriously unpretentious.

At the end of their book called *Music Hall*, Raymond Mander and Joe Mitchenson include 'The Waterman's Arms' in their index of Halls even though it's a pub. In their introduction they pose a question – 'The Waterman's Arms' in London's dockland is typical of the style of public house Music Hall of the sixties which may be the place from where the story will start all over again.'

But not for me.

The music pub and the Northern club are as close as we can get to Music Hall and later licensing hours will help. But they are not and never can be the same as the real thing.

I realize now that any attempt to revive Music Hall is impossible and foolish. Music Hall can be reproduced but it can never be revived for the simple reason that the halls have gone and the great artists like Marie Lloyd are dead.

Music Hall was unique.

Index